VAT for residential property developers and contractors

How to save VAT, maximize profits and manage the VAT
process on residential property development

Marie Stein

Foreword

Are you a property developer, contractor or professional advisor?

Are you building or converting residential properties to lease or sell?

Then you NEED to read this book.

This book has been written specially for those of you who are new to property development or construction as a business, or have limited knowledge of the VAT rules and need to know more. It includes the important VAT rules, as well as a lot of practical information about VAT and residential property development.

The book will help you to save money and manage the VAT process of your development.

If you're a developer, it will help you to maximize your profits by knowing how to keep your VAT costs down and when you can claim from HMRC.

If you're a contractor, you'll be able to save money for your customer by understanding when you can charge the zero-rate or reduced rate for your work.

And if you're a professional advisor, accountant; architect, project manager, solicitor or surveyor; you can help clients take full advantage of the VAT reliefs so that they can save money and manage the process properly.

I've avoided lots of legal jargon and legislation (unless absolutely necessary!) and there are links to HMRC guidance in case you need more detailed guidance.

And I also tell when you CAN'T save VAT on your costs or claim VAT from HMRC. If you know in advance, you can at least budget properly from the beginning and plan your expenditure accordingly.

Please start by reading the Introduction. It will help you save time in the long run!

Contents

Section 1: Introduction to VAT and important stuff you need to know

- VAT is a tax on sales of goods or services
- VAT registration
- VAT returns
- Two classes of supply:
  - Taxable and exempt
  - Three rates of "taxable" supplies: 20%, 5% and the zero-rate
- VAT recovery: the difference between taxable and exempt supplies
- Time of supply: tax points
- What "use" means in VAT
- What's your "intention"?
- "Mixed" supplies at different rates of VAT
- "Composite" supplies at one single rate

Chapter 1: Appendices

- What's an "interest" in a property?
  - Common terms: freeholds, leases etc
  - Commonholds
  - Goods or services
- Commercial properties
- Residential properties: "Qualifying properties"
- Dwellings
- What is a "dwelling"?

- o Criteria for VAT purposes
- o Conversions
- o Sales and rentals
- When developers can recover VAT on expenditure.
- Other important terms
- o "Major interest"
- o "Person constructing"
- o "Person converting"

- The facts
- o Names
- o Addresses
- o Description of property
- o Contracts and other documentation
- Keeping proper records
- What are you planning to do with the property once it's completed?
- o VAT recovery is based entirely on the <u>use</u> of the goods and services
- Understanding the commercial and legal arrangements.
- o Who's involved?
- Joint ventures
- Planning issues
- Conversions and permitted development rights
- Changing plans during the project: do you need revised consent/approval
- Always read the small print.....

- You may <u>be liable</u> to register or <u>be entitled</u> to register for VAT if your development is "in the course or furtherance of a business"
- The business <u>owner</u> is registered for VAT, not separate property developments or other business activities
- There are different rules for commercial properties and residential properties
- There are different VAT recovery methods for business and non-business developers (i.e. DIY housebuilders and converters)

Section 2: Practical stuff

- Where to start?
- Who's involved?
- Seeing the big picture
- Working out the VAT cost

- VAT and contracts
- Just because it's written down doesn't mean it's right!
- What if a contract is silent about VAT?
  - Property transactions
  - Buying opted commercial properties
- Tenanted properties
- Construction contracts
- Pricing: VAT inclusive or VAT exclusive?
- VAT related disputes
- Stamp duty land tax
- Compensation and court settlements
- Other legal documents

- The zero-rate for construction of certain new residential properties
- The reduced rate applies to certain conversions and renovations of properties for residential use, including dwellings
- There are reliefs for non-residential properties that are converted for residential use including dwellings and PROPERTY USED FOR "relevant residential purposes"
- Other VAT liabilities for residential properties
- There are limited additional VAT reliefs for alterations to residential properties for the elderly and disabled.
- Registering for VAT when you're doing residential property construction or conversions
- Commercial properties
  - Buying a new commercial property (up to 3 years old from the date of completion) is liable to VAT at 20%.

- o Subsequent sales and other income from commercial property are exempt from VAT.
- o Certain commercial property income is "excluded from exemption".
- o However commercial property owners can "opt to tax" their properties so that they can claim VAT on expenditure.

Appendix: Quick guide for working out the VAT profile of the most common developments

Section 3: The three step process

Step 1: VAT on income

- • Why is zero-rating important?
- • VAT registration
- • Sales for letting
- • When the zero-rate applies to sales
- • The conditions for zero-rating sales of converted or refurbished properties
  - o First grant
  - o Major interest
  - o Person converting
  - o Non-residential conversion
- • Does the zero-rate apply to the sale of all properties which qualified for reduced rated conversion work?
- • Don't confuse reduced rated conversion/renovation services with zero-rated converted property sales.
- • The self-contained anomoly
- • And don't confuse the ten year rule with the 2 year rule!
- • When the "new" conversion incorporates part of an existing dwelling...
- • Other issues
- • Garages
- • Sales of part completed properties
- • Relevant residential properties: certificates
- • Zero-rating sales of substantially reconstructed listed conversions

- What is a holiday let?
- Dwellings used as holiday lets
- Income from holiday lets
- Tour Operators Margin Scheme
- VAT recovery and partial exemption
- Using your own home for holiday lets

Step 2: How to save VAT on expenditure

- Why do commercial property owners have to charge VAT?
- How to buy opted commercial property VAT exempt: the VAT1614D procedure
- When can I use the VAT1614D?
- How do I do it?
  - When is the price "legally fixed"?
  - When can I issue the VAT 1614D to the vendor?
- Where do I get the form?
- Building land
- Buying as an intermediary
- The vendor's VAT position: the 2-price scenario
- Issuing certificates before the price is legally fixed
- Keep a record of the events
- What your solicitor needs to know
- Buying VAT free can reduce your stamp duty as well
- And if you have to pay VAT.....

- What if I'm buying at auction?
- Do I need planning permission for conversion work before I issue the VAT1614D?
- What happens if I'm late with my certificate?
- What if I don't use the property as intended when I bought it?
- What if the property contains an existing dwelling(s)?
- What if there are tenants in the property?
- Buying VAT exempt in other situations
- What if I'm buying a "new" commercial property to convert into a home

- How does it work in practice?
  - Consider VAT at the planning stage.
- Definitions: new construction and "qualifying properties" for conversions and renovations.
- When does the zero-rate apply?

- Reduced rate for qualifying conversions.
- Reduced rate for qualifying renovations.
- Which conversion and renovation services qualify for the reduced rate?
  - Qualifying services.

- Dwellings: conversions and renovations of the same property: the Note 3(3) issue.
- When you can save VAT on reduced rated conversion services and renovations
  - Converting horizontally
  - Converting vertically
- What's <u>always</u> standard rated even in zero-rated new construction and reduced rated qualifying conversions and renovations?
- When is "completion"?
- Mixed developments: apportioning the price between work at different rates.
  - Work done before completion
  - Work done after completion
- Garages.

- Subcontractors
  - Can subcontractors charge the reduced rate?
  - Work on "certified" properties is always standard rated
  - Does it matter whether subcontractors charge the correct VAT rate if I can claim the VAT from HMRC?
- What happens if the contractor wants to charge me 20% but I think that the 5% rate should apply?
- What if we're still unsure about the VAT liability of certain work?
- Does it matter if I can recover the VAT on my VAT return or under the DIY HouseConverters scheme?
- Surely it's cheaper using unregistered suppliers?
  - No, it's not always the cheaper option!
- Paying in cash.

- Goods and materials used in constrcution work
- What are building materials?
- Zero-rated construction and:reduced rated construction
  - New construction
  - Renovations, conversions
- Selling other stuff

- Redecoration, alterations, repairs and maintenance work
- Work carried out in the course of qualifying conversion or renovation
- Installation of energy saving insulation
- Installation of grant funded heating measures
- Adaptations for the handicapped
- Adaptations for the elderly

Step 3: When you can claim VAT from HMRC

- VAT registration for property businesses
- How and when to register for VAT
  - When you are liable to register
  - When the registration starts
  - How and when do I have to notify HMRC that I'm liable to register?
- Other types of VAT registration
  - Voluntary registration when turnover is below the registration limit
  - Registering to recover VAT on expenditure
  - Registering before making any sales
  - Group registration for associated companies
  - Exemption from registration when VAT on expenditure exceeds VAT on sales
- Place of supply rules: property and construction services
- Registration for property businesses: Form V5
- What if my sales are zero-rated and all I want to do is to claim VAT on my expenditure from HMRC?
  - Monthly VAT returns
- Claiming VAT on pre-registration expenditure
- Being VAT registered
  - Paying VAT on other income
  - Closely linked businesses
- Cancelling your registration
  - Claiming VAT on expenditure incurred after deregistration: VAT 427
- Keeping records and accounts
- Find a good accountant

- Partial exemption: why is it so difficult?
- Calculating how much VAT you can recover
- Terminology
  - Intention: First use principle
  - Direct attribution
  - Residual input tax
- The standard method
  - Income that can be excluded
  - The partial exemption year
  - Annual adjustments

- o "De minimis" limits
- o Example: Residual input tax and annual adjustments
- Special partial exemption methods
- Record keeping

- "Clawback" and "Payback": When things don't go to plan or you change your mind
  - o How does it work?
  - o How is the adjustment calculated?
    - Residential property developers
    - Recalculating directly attributed VAT
  - o Recalculation residual input tax
    - Effects on prior years' de minimis limit
- The" Capital Goods Scheme" ("CGS"): Annual adjustments reflecting actual use
  - o The CGS and property developers

- House-builders: one of the most commonly asked questions about claiming VAT
- Partial exemption for housebuilders
- VAT for property developers in the real world...........

Section 4: Other important issues for residential property developers

Introduction to the FAQs

1.1 Vanity units: 155
1.2 Electric gates and doors: 157
1.3 Integrated units: 158
1.4 Landscaping, plants, trees etc: 160

2.1 Detached garages: 164
2.2 Hiring equipment: 165
2.3 Scaffolding: 166
2.4 Plant and machinery: 167
2.5 Delivery: 167

Appendix 1: HMRC guidance

Appendix 2: Definitions of "dwelling"

About the author

Introduction

READING THIS INTRODUCTION WILL HELP YOU
SAVE VAT AND AVOID MAKING COSTLY MISTAKES.

Everybody knows that VAT and property development is a complicated subject. This book explains how VAT applies to residential property development and construction and how to calculate the actual VAT cost of your development. It's based on the fact that the VAT cost of a property is depends on 3 fundamental issues that form the 3 step process for dealing with VAT on residential property devlopment.

The "VAT cost" of a development is the difference between the amount of VAT you pay on your costs and the amount of VAT you can claim from HMRC.

It's based on the following 3 factors:

- how the finished property will be used and the VAT liability of sales or rental income;
- how much VAT you pay on your expenditure; and
- how much VAT you can claim back from HMRC.

It might seem odd that the first thing you need to know is *how the finished property will be used.* But it's important for 2 reasons:

- the type of property that you create determines how much VAT you pay on the construction work; and
- the VAT liability of income from the property determines how much VAT you can claim from HMRC.

So you have to consider all aspects to calculate the VAT cost. And as you work your way through the book, you'll see how the 3 key factors are related for VAT purposes.

To begin with, you need to know how VAT works and how it applies to residential property development. Read on over to see how the 3 step process works in practice.

Basic principles of VAT

- VAT is a tax on the sale ("supply") of goods and services, such as the freehold sale of new houses (goods) or rent from short term residential lettings (services).
- Supplies are either taxable or exempt.
- Taxable sales include sales at the standard rate: 20%, the reduced rate: 5% or the zero rate: 0%.
- Exempt sales are free from VAT.
- Businesses can claim VAT on goods and services used to make taxable sales.
- Businesses can't normally claim VAT on goods and services used to make exempt sales ("exempt input tax").

VAT and property developers

Suppose you're a property developer and you build new houses for sale and refurbish existing homes to rent on normal residential leases.

VAT liability of income

- Freehold sales of new dwellings are usually is zero-rated.
- Income from residential lets is exempt.

VAT liability of contractor's services

- Construction of new dwellings: zero-rated.
- Renovations of existing dwellings that have been empty for 2 years or more: reduced rated.

How much VAT can the developer claim?

- Sales of new homes: VAT on costs relating to the zero-rated sales of the new homes, such as professional fees, agents fees, hire of goods and building materials.
- Residential lets: the developer can't claim VAT "exempt input tax" on related costs, e.g. renovations, legal fees, agents' fees.

Of course, these are just the main principles and in practice things will depend on the specific circumstances. For example, you can claim "exempt input tax" if it falls within certain "de minimis" limits. But if you follow the 3 step approach, it will help you work out the VAT cost and manage the VAT process from the start to the end of the development.

The book is in 4 sections:

Section 1: Introduction to VAT rules and practical information that you need to know.

Chapters 1 to 4 explain how VAT works and also include lots of information that will help you deal with VAT and why it's important to pay attention to details, from putting the right name and address on documents to different meanings for the same word.

Section 2: Planning the development

Chapters 5 to 7 are about the practical side of the development. This includes explaining how it helps to see the "big picture" for VAT purposes, lots of suggestions for dealing with VAT in contracts and a summary of the main VAT and property rules.

Chapter 7 also includes a quick reference guide to help you work out the VAT profile of your development and where to find more information on specific subjects in the book.

There's also a case study that you can follow through the rest of the book to show how the technical rules work in practice.

Section 3: Main technical rules

This section includes the main technical stuff and is in 3 parts:

Chapters 8 to 9 explain the VAT liability of income from sales and rental of residential property.

Chapters 10 to 16 deal with the VAT liability of construction services, including the zero-rate, reduced rate and the confusing subject of "building materials". Chapter 10 explains how to buy commercial properties VAT free using the VAT 1614D procedure

Chapters 17 to 20 are about claiming VAT from HMRC as a VAT registered business; including the partial exemption rules and some more complex rules that may apply in later years.

Section 4: FAQs

Chapter 21 is probably one of the most important of the book: it explains when contractors/suppliers have to charge VAT on certain goods ("building materials") and services and when developers can claim the VAT charged. If you've ever been confused about vanity units, electric garage doors, landscaping, hiring plant and machinery, this is the place to start.

The rules about VAT and property are among the most difficult and there are a lot of them.

They can be just as complex for a single property conversion as a larger housing development. Understanding VAT terminology is essential. Everyday words can mean different things. For example, there are at least 3 separate definitions of "dwelling" for VAT purposes and the little 3 letter word "use" can mean different things depending on the context.

Every VAT relief is subject to certain specific requirements which are defined in the law. Seemingly minor issues can make the difference between paying no VAT at all, or at 5% or 20%.

Finally, remember that you can only ever claim VAT which has been correctly charged.   This puts an added burden on property developers because you have to understand the VAT liability of construction services to make sure that your contractors don't charge too much VAT.

Consultation: see News Flash

In March 2017, HMRC published a consultation paper about proposals to change the CIS and VAT rules for construction services. The proposal would mean that developers pay VAT on construction services to HMRC rather than to contractors - a radical change for the property and construction industry. See the News Flash for more information.

DIY property developers

If you're building a new home or converting a property into a dwelling for personal or family use, then you need my book "VAT for DIY residential property developers".

Getting advice and information from HMRC

The VAT rules about property or construction related issues are contained in a number of HMRC's VAT Notices, which are listed in Appendix One and you'll see several links to them throughout this book. The most important one is VAT Notice 708, Buildings and Construction: http://tinyurl.com/ez77v. You should use the Notices in conjunction with this book to cover all the relevant information.

Property development can be risky at the best of times, but the information this book will help you to keep your VAT costs to a minimum and help you to avoid the hassle and frustration of dealing with VAT. Just one of many important contributing factors for a successful and profitable development.

Marie

May, 2017

News Flash

IMPORTANT INFORMATION FOR THE CONSTRUCTION INDUSTRY

Proposal for business customers buying construction services

THIS COULD AFFECT CONTRACTORS, PROPERTY DEVELOPERS, OTHER BUSINESS CUSTOMERS, PROFESSIONAL ADVISORS INCLUDING ARCHITECTS, SURVEYORS, ENGINEERS, PROJECT MANAGERS

You need to know about these potential developments because they <u>will</u> affect your business

NEWS FLASH: In March 2017, HMRC issued a consultation paper with a proposal that would require business customers to deal with the VAT instead of the contractor (under a VAT "reverse charge" procedure). HMRC have explained that this is an anti-avoidance measure aimed at preventing avoidance of tax under the CIS scheme and VAT by contractors. The consultation period ends in June and you can find the consultation paper here: http://tinyurl.com/knsbvxu.

If you're a property developer, contractor, professional advisor or other business involved in the construction industry, you could be affected by the proposed new rules.

What does it mean in practice?

Under the current normal VAT rules, the contractor has to charge VAT on any construction services and/or goods that are liable to VAT at 20% or 5%. The contractor collects the VAT from the customer (usually the developer) and pays the VAT to HMRC. This is normal VAT accounting that applies to all VAT registered businesses.

Under the reverse charge procedure, the contractor won't charge any VAT. However the customer would be responsible for deciding whether any of the goods/services are liable to VAT and would have to pay this VAT directly to HMRC. The VAT can be claimed as input tax under the normal rules.

The reverse charge procedure is already used in certain other industry groups; e.g. B2B sales of mobile phones and computer chips and to collect VAT on certain services purchased from overseas businesses.

At this point, we don't know when the new rules will be introduced, how they will work in practice or even if there will be any thresholds for smaller businesses or contracts.

You can respond to HMRC's consultation paper if you have any comments, whether you're a developer, contractor or any professional advisor.

I will, of course, be monitoring developments as they happen and providing further information as and when it is available from HMRC.

But for now, it's business as usual.

Disclaimer

This book is an introduction to the subject of VAT and residential property developments, based on my interpretation of the legislation and HMRC guidance at the date of publication. It DOES NOT cover every possible scenario nor does it replace formal advice on specific situations. Please take proper advice to be certain about the VAT implications of your development and avoid unexpected VAT issues along the way.

The main VAT rules are summarized for the purposes of this book and their relevance to residential property developers. Links to HMRC's guidance on the subjects discussed in this book are included throughout the book and you must refer to their guidance for full and detailed information about any subject.

Marie Stein

August, 2017

Legislation and caselaw

Legislation

You will find relevant VAT legislation listed at the beginning of each of the technical chapters of this book. If you want to look at any specific part of the legislation, you should be able to find it online at http://www.legislation.gov.uk/.

Otherwise, the information provided in this book is based on my own interpretation of the VAT legislation as it exists at the date of publication. I tend to take a reasonably cautious approach, while recommending sensible and practical VAT planning to help businesses to be VAT efficient. Please let me know if you don't agree with my interpretation or if you've received contradicting rulings from HMRC.

I've included links to HMRC's notices and occasionally HMRC's staff manuals throughout the book so you can refer to their guidance for more information.   All of this information is available on HMRC's website www.hmrc.gov.uk.

Caselaw

Property and construction are among the most common of appeal subjects in UK and there have been literally hundreds, if not thousands, of cases about different aspects of UK VAT law relating to property and construction. Some of these decisions have caused HMRC to change their interpretation of the law and adopt a different policy.

Changes in policy as a result of caselaw or consultation with the business community are usually reflected in HMRC's public notices. You should always make sure that you're reading the most up to date versions of HMRC's notices in case there have been any changes in HMRC's policy since this book was issued.

Chapter 1

How VAT works

This chapter explains the basic rules about VAT.

- VAT is a tax on sales of goods or services
- VAT registration
- VAT returns
- Two classes of supply
  - Taxable and exempt
  - Three rates of "taxable" supplies: 20%, 5% and the zero-rate
- Claiming VAT: the difference between taxable and exempt supplies
  - Special rule for "building materials"; vanity units etc
  - Plant hire, scaffolding and other services
- Time of supply: tax points
- What "use" means in VAT
- What's your "intention"?
- "Mixed" supplies at different rates of VAT
- "Composite" supplies at one single rate

There's more information in HMRC's "Introduction to VAT" http://tinyurl.com/nqtcmy and VAT Notice 700: The VAT Guide: http://tinyurl.com/9ykqw is HMRC's main reference book which explains the main principles of VAT in some depth. VAT Notice 708: Buildings and construction http://tinyurl.com/mod94mc is the most important notice for contractors and developers.

Even if you think you understand how VAT works, please take the time to read this chapter.

I get a lot of queries from contractors and developers who spend ages looking for answers in Notice 708, when the real problem is that they don't understand the basic VAT rules work. It's a bit like trying to change gear when you don't know how to start a car.

Please note that I'll use the following terms during this book:

A "developer" is someone who builds new property or converts or refurbishes existing property.

"Contractors" are those engaged by the developer to carry out the conversion work.

VAT on sales and purchases

A supply is the sale of goods or services.

VAT is charged on sales of goods and services done or given for a "consideration".

A supply includes sales, leases and licences to use or occupy a property.

Consideration is generally any sort of payment, usually cash, but sometimes it might be in the form of goods or services given in return in a barter transaction.

Sales of goods and services are "ouputs" and the VAT charged is "output tax".

Purchases of goods and services are "inputs" and the VAT paid is "input tax".

I'll use the terms "sales" and "purchases" throughout this book to keep the technical jargon to a minimum, but I'll use the term "supply" if necessary when discussing specific technical issues.

VAT Registration

The business owner is registered for VAT; whether it's a limited company, a partnership, sole proprietor or any other legal entity

Business owners must apply to register for VAT if the value of their taxable sales in any past 12 month or future thirty day period exceeds the VAT registration limit, which is currently £85,000 (May 2017). This limit is increased each year, usually in line with inflation, so check the HMRC website for current limits. There are penalties for failing to notify HMRC that you're liable to register at the right time. See Chapter 17 for more information.

You can also register for VAT on a voluntary basis if the value of your taxable sales is below this limit. The VAT registration covers all of the business activities of the business owner.

VAT Returns

VAT registered businesses submit VAT returns and payments, usually every 3 months. HMRC can issue penalties if either returns or payments are submitted late.

VAT registered businesses include VAT on sales and expenditure made in the period covered by the VAT return and pay the difference to HMRC. If your input tax is higher than your output tax, you can submit a repayment return and HMRC will refund the difference.

Two classes of supply for VAT purposes: taxable and exempt

Taxable sales

Most sales of goods and services are liable to VAT at one of three rates currently in force:

- Standard rate: 20%
- Reduced rate: 5%
- Zero rate: 0%

ALL sales of goods and services in the UK are liable to VAT at 20%, unless the law specifically says otherwise.

In the case of residential properties, the reduced rate applies to certain conversion and renovation work, as explained in Chapter 12.

The second class of supplies are known as exempt supplies

EXEMPT supplies are not liable to VAT.

Claiming VAT: the difference between zero-rated and exempt supplies

As explained above, the main difference between taxable and exempt supplies is as follows:

- Businesses making taxable supplies at any rate – including zero rated residential property sales - can claim input tax on goods and services used to make those supplies apart from certain specific costs which are explained in Chapter 17 ("blocked input tax").
- Businesses making exempt supplies can't normally claim input tax on goods and services used to make those supplies. This VAT is called "exempt input tax".

> People often use the terms "VAT exempt"or "VAT free"or "VAT zero-rated" without understanding what they mean. Because the distinction between zero-rated and exempt is very important, I've made a point of using the correct terminology throughout the book to avoid any confusion.

It's particularly important for residential property developers to understand the distinction between "exempt" supplies and "zero-rated" supplies. Income from residential lets is normally exempt from VAT so landlords have to factor VAT that they can't claim into their budgeting.

If all your income is taxable, you can claim most or all of your input tax VAT from HMRC. However <u>you can only claim VAT that has been *correctly charged*</u>, so make sure that you don't pay more VAT than you should; e.g. for contractors' services that are eligible for the reduced rate or the zero-rate.

- Special rules for "building materials": vanity units, integrated appliances, landscaping...

All of those problems about when you can claim VAT on vanity units, integrated appliances, landscaping, garage doors..........

Most property developers and contractors will have come across the issue of "building materials" at some point. The rule exists to ensure that the zero-rate and reduced rate only applies to certain goods and materials (i.e. "building materials") supplied and incorporated during the course of construction, conversion or renovation by building contractors.

Also, property developers can't claim VAT on these goods (and in some cases the labour for installing the goods) even if they are making zero-rated sales of the new or converted properties.

I've explained the issue in more detail in <u>Chapter 15</u> and dealt with some of the most common FAQs in <u>Chapter 21,</u> Part 1, explaining when contractors have to charge VAT and when developers can claim VAT.

- Plant hire, scaffolding and other services

Another area of confusion is VAT on certain other related services, including hire of plant and machinery and scaffolding. In <u>Chapter 21,</u> Part 2, I've discussed some of the most common FAQs about these issues.

Time of supply: tax point

The "time of supply" or "tax point" is the date on which a supply of goods or services is deemed to take place. If, for example, you sell goods on 1 November, then the tax point is 1 November and you include the VAT on that sale on the VAT return which includes the month of November and pay the VAT to HMRC.

The basic "tax point" for sales of goods is when the goods are delivered to customers.

The basic "tax point" for sales of services is when the services are completed.

However these "basic tax points" are normally over-ridden by other commercial events, usually the date on which the customer pays or the date on which the supplier issues a VAT invoice. See VAT Notice 700, sections 14 and 15 for more information http://tinyurl.com/n9ysdj9.

And there are special rules for certain land and property transactions and for services carried out by contractors or sub-contractors in the construction industry, including the authenticated receipt procedure and self-billing. See VAT Notice 708, paragraph 23 http://tinyurl.com/l5vbl7v.

"Use" in VAT

The word "use" is one of the most common in the English language. Whether it's describing how we're going to "use" our week off work to decorate the house or whether we'll be "using" our newly converted property as an investment property or to sell. It's a commonly used word, whether as a verb or a noun.

However the word has two specific meanings for VAT purposes.

How much VAT you can claim: In some circumstances, property developers can register for VAT and claim VAT on development expenditure. In this context, "use" means whether the goods and/or services that a business purchases will be "used" to make either taxable or exempt supplies.

As explained above, you can't normally claim VAT on expenditure if the goods or services will be used to make exempt supplies. However VAT on goods and services can be claimed if you're using the goods and services to make taxable sales.

For example, income from sales or lettings of newly converted dwellings can fall into any one of three categories. The property could be sold by the developer as a zero-rated sale. It could be used for residential lettings, generating exempt rental income or let out for holiday accommodation, which is standard rated.

That's three different VAT liabilities of income according to how one single property will be used: two of them taxable and the other exempt. So the principle of "use" is important throughout this book as it defines whether or not you can claim VAT on expenditure.

How will finished properties be used? In this second context, "use" refers to the physical purpose of the property; i.e. who will occupy the property and it's normal day to day use. For example, conversion services only qualify for the reduced rate if the finished property will be used as a dwelling or for some other type of residential purpose, such as a residential home for the elderly.

Other "uses"

The word also comes up in respect of other VAT issues such as business or non-business <u>use</u> of assets; <u>use</u> for charitable purposes, so you have to be aware of the context in which certain every day words or phrases are used.

But for the most part in this book, we'll be concerned about the two situations explained above; i.e. whether goods or services will be USED to make taxable or exempt sales; and who will USE i.e. occupy the property and for what purpose.

What's your "intention"?

The word "intention" is also important. When you incur expenditure used for business purposes, you have to establish whether you <u>intend</u> to use the goods or services to generate taxable or exempt sales. The income might be generated in the same week, month, year or even later, particularly in the case of property developments. However you have to know at the time you incur the expense so that you know whether or not you can claim the VAT.

There are also rules that require businesses to adjust the amount of VAT originally claimed <u>in future years</u>. They apply <u>if the actual use is different to the original intention or the actual use changes from the initial use</u> over time, for example, if you rent dwellings on short term leases instead of selling them. They are called the "change of intention or use" or "payback/clawback" rules and the "capital goods scheme" and are explained in <u>Chapter 19</u>.

They are complex rules but it's important to be aware of them if you're a property developer.

Mixed developments at different rates of VAT

An important principle in VAT is the concept of "mixed supplies" (sometimes called "multiple supplies") This is when two or more goods or services, which are part of the same contract/order and billed for a single amount, are liable to VAT at the different rates. This often happens in the case of property development, especially where the contractor is carrying out construction work on mixed developments, which could include zero-rated new construction services, reduced rate qualifying conversion work and standard rated extensions and alterations.

What does this mean?

It means that the contractor has to apportion his price between the different elements of the work, itemizing those elements that are liable to VAT at the different rates on the invoice and charging VAT on the different elements at the appropriate rate.

If the supplier can't itemize the different elements properly, then everything covered by the invoice is liable to VAT at the standard rate. If you can't claim the VAT because you'll be receiving exempt rental income, it's important that your contractor identifies work carried out at the different rates and charges the correct rate for the amounts charged to keep your VAT costs as low as possible.

HMRC's guidance about apportionment is in VAT Notice 700, section 8.1 http://tinyurl.com/9ykqw which explains how suppliers can apportion their invoices when making mixed supplies. There are further references throughout Notice 708; Buildings and construction, in particular section 16 which explains how apportionment applies to property and construction http://tinyurl.com/q6wz4vl.

Composite supplies at one single rate

The opposite to "mixed supplies" is the concept of "composite supplies". A composite supply is where a supply comprises a number of individual elements which individually have different VAT liabilities.

However, unlike mixed supplies, there is *one primary element and the other elements are regarded as being ancillary to the main element and only "for the better enjoyment" of the main element.*

For example, when you buy a new washing machine, you usually receive an instruction book. Books and leaflets are normally zero-rated, so if sold separately, then the book would be zero-rated. However when sold with the washing machine, it is "for the better enjoyment" of the main element; i.e. to help you use the washing machine, so the whole supply is liable at the standard rate as a composite supply.

The concept of composite supply can be relevant in the construction industry; for example contractors may make composite supplies in design and build contracts. Instead of the developer employing architects and other professional advisors, or hiring goods direct. where all of which are liable to 20% VAT, all of the goods and services are supplied to the main contractor who can make a single zero-rated or reduced rated supply of construction services. See VAT Notice 708, section 3.4 for more information http://tinyurl.com/mdc8465.

Chapter One: Checklist

- There are two classes of supplies – or sales – for VAT purposes: taxable and exempt. Sales of goods and services are "outputs".
- VAT is charged on taxable sales of goods or services by VAT registered businesses at 20%, 5% or zero-rated. This is "output tax".
- Purchases of goods and services are "inputs" and VAT on them is "input tax."
- The main difference between taxable and exempt sales is that businesses making exempt supplies normally can't recover VAT on related expenditure. Businesses making taxable supplies can recover VAT on expenditure, with certain exceptions.
- Sales and rentals of residential property are either zero-rated or exempt.
- "Use" means both the practical use or occupancy of the property and whether goods or services are used to make taxable or exempt supplies.
- "Composite" and "mixed" supplies both include two or more elements that have different VAT liabilities. Composite supplies have one primary element while mixed supplies contain a number of equally important parts.

VAT Invoices

The following is an extract from HMRC VAT Notice 700, The VAT Guide, paragraph 16.3

http://tinyurl.com/p97npe7

Information needed on full VAT invoice:

- *a sequential number based on one or more series which uniquely identifies the document*
- *the time of the supply (tax point)*
- *the date of issue of the document (where different to the time of supply)*
- *your name, address and VAT registration number - you may issue invoices under a trading name, but your legal name and address details must still be shown somewhere on the document*
- *the name and address of the person (customer) to whom the goods or services have been supplied*
- *a description sufficient to identify the goods or services supplied*
- *for each description, the quantity of the goods or the extent of the services, and the rate of VAT and the amount payable, excluding VAT, expressed in any currency*
- *the gross total amount payable, excluding VAT, expressed in any currency*
- *the rate of any cash discount offered*
- *the total amount of VAT chargeable, expressed in sterling*
- *the unit price*
- *the reason for any zero rate or exemption*

The final bullet point refers to the following types of supply:

- *supplies subject to a second-hand margin scheme*
- *supplies subject to the TOMS*
- *intra-EU exempt supplies*
- *intra-EU reverse charge supplies*
- *intra-EU zero-rated supplies*

The VAT fractions

Usually, retail prices are shown as VAT inclusive amounts. We call this the "gross selling price." The VAT exclusive selling price is called the "net selling price". Building contractors usually give VAT exclusive prices, which means that they add the VAT rate once you've agreed the price.

However, retailers don't have to show the VAT if the gross value of the sale is £250 or less. The VAT fraction is the VAT proportion of the gross price.

If you're preparing a DIY Refund Scheme claim, some of your invoices will only show gross prices, so you have to calculate the amount of VAT included, by using the VAT fraction as explained below.

Goods or services that are standard rated: 20/120

Suppose you buy a new table for £200. The standard rate of VAT is currently 20%.

The gross sales price always includes VAT, so your £200 is made up of 2 parts:

• the net (VAT exclusive) sales price which for the purposes of the VAT fraction is 100%; and
• the VAT amount which is the net sales price multiplied by the VAT rate; in this case 20%.

In percentage terms, this means that the gross selling price is 120% of the net sales price and the VAT included is 20% of the gross selling price. The gross price of the table is £200; i.e. 120% of the net price.

VAT included in the gross price is calculated as *20/120 x £200 = £33.67*.

The fraction can also be shown as 1/6.

Goods or services that are reduced rate: 5/105

If you buy a child's car seat, including VAT at 5%, for £50 gross, then the calculation is as follows:

£50 = 100% net price + 5% VAT = 105%

VAT included in the gross price is calculated as *5/105 x £50 = £2.38.*

The faction can also be shown as 1/21.

Chapter 2

VAT and properties: the important terminology

This chapter introduces the main terminology which applies to VAT and properties and the definitions which I'll be using throughout this book. I'd suggest you have a quick read through then refer back when you need to know more about specific words or terms.

You need to understand these terms because they define important principles in VAT legislation.

The most important terms are as follows:

- What's an "interest" in a property?
  - Common terms: freeholds, leases etc.
  - Commonhold
  - Goods or services
- Commercial properties
- Residential properties: "Qualifying properties"
- Dwellings
  - What is a "dwelling"?
  - Criteria for VAT purposes
- Conversions
- Sales and rentals
  - When developers can claim VAT on expenditure.
- Other important terms
  - "Major interest"
  - "Person constructing"
  - "Person converting"

There is a comprehensive glossary of terms relating to property and construction in HMRC's VAT Notice 708 "Buildings and Construction", section 14 http://tinyurl.com/nkkw2lk.

One of the most important is the word "dwelling", because it means different things according to the context. The main principles are discussed in this chapter. Appendix 2 of this book lists the main criteria of each definition and when each definition applies

What's an "interest" in property?

Property includes both land, buildings and civil engineering works, such as road, bridges etc.

An "interest" in land is the legal term that applies to any type of property transaction. Owners of land or property will normally "grant an interest" to a purchaser or tenant. An "interest" can include freeholds, leases, licences to occupy and rights over land; for example:

- The freeholder of any property owns the property in the same way as any other asset, e.g. a car or a television etc, not just the right to occupy it.
- Property owners can grant interests such as leases or licences to others to occupy or use their property.
- Anyone who holds an interest in a property can grant a lesser interest to others as long as the landlord. For example, if I own a 99 year lease over an apartment, I could sublet the property by granting a shorter sublease to my own tenant.

Other common land transactions include:

- Surrender – when a tenant surrenders the remaining term on his lease to the landlord.
- Assignment – when a tenant assigns the remaining term on his lease to a third party.
- Premium – usually the initial payment made by a tenant to the landlord on the granting of a lease, followed by monthly or quarterly rental payments.
- Licences to occupy, rights over property, rights of way.

Most income from property sales, lettings or other interests is exempt from VAT; including freehold sales, leases and the other arrangements mentioned above. The VAT liability of the most common forms of income from both residential and commercial property is listed in Chapter 5.

Commonhold

A "commonhold" gives owners of parts of a building, occupied in common, a freehold interest in their respective parts. An example would be a block of flats, where individuals own the "commonhold" of their flats.

Commonholds can also apply to commercial property or part commercial/part residential.

The VAT treatment of work on and supplies of such properties normally follows the same rules as those applying to freeholds. However there are some specific issues that only apply to commonhold properties, so you must refer to HMRC's guidance for more detailed information.

HMRC's guidance about commonholds is in VAT Notice 742: Land and property, section 13: http://tinyurl.com/o53aotd.

Goods or services?

The sale of the freehold or a long lease in land or property are called "major interests" (see next page) and are treated as sales of goods for VAT purposes.

Other property transactions are called "minor interests" and are treated as sales of services for VAT purposes.

The VAT liabilities for grants of "major interests" and "minor interests" can be different; for example the freehold sale of a new property by the developer is zero-rated, while leasing the property on a short-term residential let is standard rated. We'll be discussing these issues throughout the book.

Commercial properties

The term "commercial property" doesn't appear in VAT law. However we use the term whenever we're referring to properties that aren't residential properties. I've explained the meaning of "residential properties" below (section 2.3).

I've listed the important VAT rules relating to commercial and residential property for VAT purposes in Chapter 7.

Residential properties: "Qualifying properties"

Most of us use the term "residential" to refer to any sort of home or dwelling or residential home. It's the term normally used by property developers and local authorities.

However VAT legislation uses the term "residential" in a slightly different context, as explained below:

- Dwellings: single household dwellings, including houses, flats, bungalows and mansions and multi-occupancy dwellings.
- Properties used for "relevant residential purposes": multi-occupancy dwellings, such as HMOs and residential homes.
- Properties used for "relevant charitable purposes". These are properties used by charities for non-business charitable activities, or community properties for non-business use such as local village halls.

These are called "qualifying properties" for VAT purposes.

The VAT law provides a number of reliefs for dwellings, properties used for "relevant residential purposes" and "relevant charitable purposes".

> Throughout this book, I've used the word "residential" in a broader sense, to include dwellings; relevant residential properties and relevant charitable properties. I use the word "dwelling" to refer to single household dwellings including houses and flats, unless otherwise stated.

Dwellings

There are three definitions of the word "dwelling" in the VAT legislation.

There is also a further category of "multi-occupancy dwelling", such as bedsits.

What is a "dwelling"?

The definitions of "dwelling" include conditions about their physical attributes and restrictions on the sale or occupancy of the dwelling. But these don't actually deal with the <u>purpose</u> of a <u>dwelling</u> and what distinguishes a dwelling from other living accommodation.

HMRC's current definition of a "home" as "a place where one lives, regarding and treating it as home."

This distinguishes a "dwelling" from other uses, such as holiday accommodation or temporary shelter. It suggests that the property is used on a permanent basis and is the primary place of residence for the occupants. However the word can also apply to properties used as second homes or even holiday homes, as long as they meet the conditions included in the definitions set out below.

Definitions for VAT purposes

Factors common to all three definitions

The definitions are similar in many respects with slight differences.

They all contain the following four basic conditions:

- the dwelling consists of self-contained living accommodation;
- there is no provision for direct internal access from the dwelling to any other dwelling or part of a dwelling;

- the separate use of the dwelling is not prohibited by the terms of any covenant, statutory planning consent or similar provision; and
- the separate disposal of the dwelling is not prohibited by the terms of any covenant, statutory planning consent or similar provision.

I've explained the differences between the three types of "dwelling" and "multi-purpose dwellings" below. The legal definitions are in Appendix 2.

"Designed as a dwelling or number of dwellings"

This is the definition that applies to most dwellings. In addition to the four basic conditions, it includes the following additional condition:

"statutory planning consent has been granted in respect of that dwelling and its construction or conversion has been carried out in accordance with that consent".

It applies in the context of:

- Zero- rated construction work. See Chapter 11.
- Zero-rated sales of new dwellings. See Chapter 8.
- Zero-rated sales of converted non-residential dwellings. See Chapter 8.
- DIY House Builders or HomeConverters Refund Scheme for people who build or convert their own dwelling for personal or family use.

The additional condition means that the developer must have received planning consent for the construction of the property concerned and that the work has been carried out to the specifications given in the planning consent.

See VAT Notice 708, section 14.2 for HMRC's comments about this definition: http://tinyurl.com/pmyorhm.

"Designed to remain as or become a dwelling or number of dwellings"

This definition contains only the four basic conditions. It is used to define listed residential dwellings and the conditions must be met if developers intend to sell reconstructed listed properties under the rules explained in Chapter 8.

See VAT Notice 708, section 14.3 for HMRC's guidance about this definition: http://tinyurl.com/k45o73b.

"Single household dwelling"

In addition to the four basic conditions, a single household dwelling must also meet the following additional condition:

"is designed for occupation by a single household either as a result of having been originally constructed for that purpose (and has not been subsequently adapted for occupation of any other kind), or as a result of adaptation...".

The reduced rate for conversions and renovations of dwellings ONLY applies when the result of the work is to change the number of single household dwellings in a property or for the renovation of single household dwellings as explained in Chapter 12.

To qualify for the reduced rate of VAT on construction work, conversions must change the number of single household dwellings in an existing property.

See VAT Notice 708, section 14.4 for HMRC's guidance http://tinyurl.com/q4p3hp6.

"Multi-occupancy" dwelling includes the following additional requirements:

- "is designed for occupation by persons not forming a single household either as a result of having been originally constructed for that purpose (and has not been subsequently adapted for occupation of any other kind), or as a result of adaptation;
- is not to any extent used for a relevant residential purpose...".

The term normally refers to bedsits or similar dwellings which qualify for reduced rated conversions. Conversions of existing properties into new MODs qualify for the reduced rate as explained in Chapter 12.

See HMRC's guidance 708, section 14.5 for HMRC's guidance http://tinyurl.com/kpkolxs.

The full legal definitions of the terms "dwelling", "single household dwelling", property used for "relevant residential purposes" and "relevant charitable purposes" are included in Appendix 1.

Conversions

There are 2 separate definitions of "conversion":

- the first type of conversion means that the work may qualify for the reduced rate of VAT;

- the second type of conversion means that the sale of the property may be zero-rated and is also the definition that must be met to qualify for a VAT refund under the DIY VAT Refund Scheme.

I've explained more about the definitions of the terms and how they are used in the appendix to this chapter.

Sales and rentals

Most income from the sale or rental of residential properties is exempt from VAT, which means that the vendor or landlord usually can't claim VAT on the construction or conversion expenditure or any other related expenditure. This means that <u>if you're converting or refurbishing dwellings, you'll need sufficient funding to pay for the VAT inclusive expenditure of the development</u>, especially if seeking finance to fund the project, for example when putting together a business plan or applying for a loan.

When developers can claim VAT on expenditure

There are, however, three situations when property developers <u>can</u> claim VAT on the cost of either constructing or converting residential property, <u>because the income from the sale or lease is zero-rated</u>.

These are as follows:

- The first grant of a "major interest" in the property by the "person constructing" new residential properties: zero-rated.
- The first grant of a "major interest" in the property by the "person converting" new residential properties from non-residential properties: zero-rated.
- The first grant of a "major interest" in a substantially reconstructed listed residential property by the "person reconstructing": zero-rated.

These terms are defined below. See <u>Chapter 8</u> for more details about the zero-rated sales of new residential properties, converted non-residential properties and reconstructed residential properties.

Other important terms

"Major interest"

This means either the sale of the freehold or a lease in excess of 21 years; or in Scotland the estate or interest or a lease of not less than 20 years.

It includes the sale, assignment or surrender any of the following interests:

- the freehold;
- in England, Wales and Northern Ireland, a lease for a term certain exceeding 21 years;
- in Scotland, the estate or interest of the owner; or
- in Scotland, the tenant's interest under a lease for a term of not less than 20 years.

For the purposes of this book, I'll refer to sales of freeholds or long leases.

"Person constructing, "person converting" and "person reconstructing"

These terms are legal definitions which normally apply to residential property developers who have either constructed new properties, converted existing properties or reconstructed listed properties.   In order to zero-rate the grant of a "major interest", one of the conditions is that the property owner must meet the conditions of "person constructing, "person converting" and "person reconstructing". See Chapter 8 for more information.

Chapter 2: Checklist

- Properties broadly fall into two categories for VAT purposes; commercial and residential.
- Residential includes dwellings, relevant residential use and relevant charitable use properties. These terms are defined in the law.
- There are two definitions of "conversion", one applies to reduced rated conversion work on certain residential properties; the other to zero-rated sales of certain converted residential properties.
- There are three separate definitions of "dwelling".
- Zero-rating applies to certain property sales which fulfil the criteria as explained in Chapter 8.

Chapter 2: Appendix

So what exactly IS a conversion?

I've mentioned in that certain words have specific definitions according to the context. Two of the most important in this context are "dwelling" and "conversion".

There are at least 3 different definitions of "dwelling" and 2 different definitions of "conversion".

The definitions of "dwelling" are explained in detail in HMRC's VAT Notice 708, paragraph 14 http://tinyurl.com/otedchh and the criteria are listed in Appendix 2. While they are similar, there are slightly different criteria for different issues, meaning that the criteria for zero-rating construction of new dwellings and for reduced-rated renovation and conversion services are slightly different. I've explained each definition of "conversion" or "dwelling" in the relevant chapters in this book so you know which applies to your situation.

- Conversions
- Reduced rated conversions
- Zero-rated sales
- In practice
- And it's not just VAT...

Conversions

In this chapter, I'm focusing on the 2 definitions of the word "conversion". As I mentioned above, one definition applies to reduced rated conversion and renovation services, the other for the DIY home-converters scheme.

This means that while your conversion may qualify for reduced rated conversion services, the sale of your converted property may not qualify for the zero-rate, which means you can't claim VAT on your costs.

As I've explained below, it primarily concerns how the properties were used BEFORE the conversion.

Conversions that qualify for 5% contractors services

These include conversions of the following properties:

- *a property that has never been lived in, such as an office block or a barn*

- *a multiple occupancy building such as a bedsit block*
- *living accommodation which is not self-contained, such as a pub containing staff accommodation that is not self-contained*
- *any dwelling which had previously been adapted in its entirety to another use, such as to offices or a dental practice*

Extract from VAT Notice 708, s7.3: http://tinyurl.com/po66ewb

Conversions that qualify for the zero-rate when sold by the person converting

The conversion must qualify as a "non-residential conversions"

- *The building (or the part being converted) was never "used as a dwelling" before OR has not been used as such within the 10 years immediately prior to the conversion.*
- *It does NOT include buildings that have been "used as a dwelling" such as:*
  - *public houses and shops where any private living accommodation for the landlord, owner, manager or staff is not self-contained - normally because part of the living accommodation, such as the kitchen, is contained within the commercial areas rather than the private areas*
  - *bed-sit accommodation, and*
  - *crofts*

- *The conversion must be a "non-residential conversion" which includes:*
  - *a commercial building (such as an office, warehouse, shop)*
  - *an agricultural building (such as a barn), or*
  - *a redundant school or church*
  into a building which is 'designed as a dwelling or number of dwellings'.

Extracts from VAT Notice 708, paragraph 5 http://tinyurl.com/mdc8465and VAT431C: http://tinyurl.com/pt9ec7h

What's the difference in practice?

It's mainly to do with how the buildings were used before the conversion.

- To qualify for reduced rate conversion services, there must be a change in the number of "single household dwellings" as a result of the conversion.

- To qualify for zero-rating as a sale, the conversion must be a "non-residential conversion" which means that the property must not have been lived in or "used as a dwelling" in the previous 10 years.

The distinction between "single household dwelling" and "used as a dwelling" is the important issue.

A good example would be a pub, which has some private accommodation, e.g. bedrooms and a bathroom, but isn't self-contained.   Suppose a manager and his family lived in those rooms before the conversion.

- The conversion of all or part of the property into a "single household dwelling" would qualify for reduced rate contractors' services .

- However, because the property has been <u>"used as a dwelling"</u> within the prior 10 years means that the new owner can't claim any VAT under the DIY refund scheme.

We'll be looking at these issues in more detail in <u>Chapter 8</u> (conversions for sale) and <u>Chapter 12</u> (reduced rate for conversion services).

And it's not just VAT...

Finally, a lot of words that are used in the VAT legislation have different definitions for non-VAT purposes. A good example is the word "occupied" for the purposes of the "empty home" rules is probably different to that used for planning purposes.

Just be sure to keep checking this book if you're confused about the definitions for VAT purposes in different circumstances.

Conversion: Checklist

- It's really important to understand the correct definition of certain words, particularly "dwelling" and "conversion", because the rules use different terms according to the context.
- The most important distinction is between a "single household dwelling" and "used as a dwelling".
- The criteria to qualify for reduced rate construction services are less onerous than the criteria for the DIY refund scheme.
- To qualify for the DIY refund scheme, the conversion must be a "non-residential conversion" which means not used a dwelling in the previous 10 years.
- Commercial property developers may also benefit from the reliefs and can register for VAT to claim VAT on costs if their conversion is a "non-residential conversion".

Chapter 3

Why it's so important to pay attention to the details

One of the main reasons that people end up with VAT problems is because they don't pay proper attention to details. I've seen several examples over the years where even large businesses have made basic errors – such as getting the names wrong on documentation – costing them thousands or tens of thousands of pounds in unexpected VAT expenditure.

In this chapter, I've summarized the important facts that you must get right to avoid VAT problems.

- The facts
  - Names
  - Address
  - Description of property
  - Contracts and other documentation
- Keeping proper records
- Understanding the commercial and legal arrangements: the "chain of supply".
- Who's involved?
- Use consistent terminology for the parties involved
- A special mention about joint ventures
- Planning issues
  - Conversions and permitted development rights
  - When plans change after the work commences
- Always read the small print.....

The facts

The most important facts that MUST be correct on all documents:

- **Names**.

Make that the correct names are shown on all documents and preferably in a consistent format; especially contracts, leases and VAT invoices and other legal documents. Whether you're registered for VAT or making a DIY Refund Scheme claim, it's ESSENTIAL that purchase invoices are issued to the correct legal person or you won't be able to claim VAT from HMRC.

- **Addresses.**

Ensure that the correct postal address and post code is shown on all documents.

- **Description of property.**

Make sure that the correct and full description of the property is contained on all documents. Compare with the information on planning applications and other legal documents to ensure consistency.

- **Contracts and other documentation**

Check all legal documents to make sure that the correct information is shown and ask your solicitor to make any necessary changes if the facts are incorrect. Make sure that all relevant documents are signed and dated by the relevant parties.

Keeping proper records

Set up a filing system for all documents relating to the development. If you're submitting VAT returns, make sure that you have correct VAT invoices to support VAT repayments. See HMRC VAT Notice 700/20: Keeping VAT records http://tinyurl.com/cnlqa43 for information about retaining records for VAT purposes.

If there is more than one version of a document, find out which one is valid and keep a signed copy available for inspection by VAT officers. See Chapter 6 for more information about dealing with VAT issues in contracts.

Understanding the legal and commercial arrangements: the "chain of supply"

It's important to understand both the technical terms, the commercial arrangements and the roles of the various parties involved in the project to get the VAT right. I've seen many situations go wrong because the parties get confused about "who is doing what for whom". So it's worth taking time at the beginning to get things right.

The term "chain of supply" defines the sales of goods and services from one person to another.

Who's involved?

So in a typical property conversion development, the arrangement would be:

- A property developer buys a property.
- The property developer engages suppliers to provide various services:

- o   a solicitor to do the legal work
  - o   an architect to design the conversion;
  - o   and a contractor to carry out the conversion.
- The developer then rents the newly converted dwelling to tenants as an investment property or sells it outright.

In each of the above scenarios, one party is selling something to someone else, whether it's the initial property purchase, the solicitor or architect providing professional services, the contractor doing the conversion work, or the developer who rents or sells the property. So the "chain of supply" for the ownership of the property would be from the original vendor to Dev Co to the purchaser.

In most property developments, the picture is a lot more complicated, because there are several parties involved, as illustrated in Chapter 5.

Solicitors can be an invaluable source of information if you need to confirm any facts. Whenever I'm working with an accountant or a client on a property project, I always recommend asking the solicitor to confirm the contractual details to ensure that I and the client both have a full picture of the "chain of supply".

Joint ventures.

Joint venture arrangements can cover a variety of arrangements. Typical examples include those where two or more parties come together to finance a project, or where one party provides finance while the other provides services. Sometimes it's a combination of these types of arrangements.

If you're considering doing any sort of property development involving a joint venture, PLEASE take professional advice about the commercial arrangements and legal structure before you start. Over the years I've been asked to sort out many VAT problems encountered by joint ventures and in nearly every case, some thought and sensible planning in advance could have avoided all of the problems and saved the developers a lot of time and money.

Even large businesses can be confused about these situations because they've not fully thought through the legal and commercial arrangements, never mind the VAT implications.

HMRC often treat such "joint ventures" as partnerships for VAT purposes, albeit that there is no formal partnership or partnership treatment for tax purposes. Either way, it should be possible to structure the legal and commercial a arrangements in a way which works for VAT, but you need to sort this all out at the beginning of the project to avoid problems.

Planning issues

Planning consents and other similar requirements are an integral parts of the VAT process.

One of the most important requirements to qualify for the zero-rate, reduced rate conversion services or to claim VAT under the DIY refund scheme is that the construction work has both required and received appropriate building consent and/or planning permission.

You must have building consent, planning permission and any other regulatory authority BEFORE your contractor starts working, or your contractor will have to charge 20% VAT.

This is very important, because the law says that the reduced rate for conversions and renovations only applies *if any statutory planning consent and statutory building control approval that may be needed has been granted.* The definitions that include these requirements are in Appendix 2.

You need to have any such consents, permissions and approvals *before the construction work begins*; otherwise the work will be liable to 20% VAT. HMRC have assessed many contractors for VAT on new construction, conversions and refurbishments and the Tribunals and Courts invariably agree with HMRC. This is an important issue so wait until you have any necessary consents etc even if you're impatient to start working on the property.

Conversions and permitted development rights

Some conversions don't require full planning permission/consent, but are allowed under the new "Permitted development rights" ("PDR") rules. In this case, HMRC will accept alternative documentary evidence. This is explained in Business Brief 9/2016: http://tinyurl.com/jmunuan.

PDRs apply to conversions of certain existing commercial properties into dwellings. PDR developments qualify for reduced rate conversion services and the DIY home-converters scheme as long as the owner has the alternative documentary evidence.

What happens if you change plans during the project: do you need revised consent/approval?

There's one further VERY IMPORTANT point about the subject of planning. Sometimes your plans change during the course of the project and you need revised planning permission, usually from your local planning authority, before you can proceed with the change of plans.

If this happens*, it's essential that you obtain proper planning permission for the revised plans or the work won't qualify for the reduced rate or zero-rate.* The original consent/approval only covers the original plans and you must have the revised consent/approval or your contractor will have to charge VAT at 20% on at least part of their work.

I've come across situations where people didn't realise that they needed revised consent/approval for such work when plans change during the construction process and HMRC has issued assessments to the contractors for under-charged VAT. Don't let this happen to you. Make sure you check with the planning office and get revised consent if you need it or ask for written confirmation that you don't need revised consent.

Always read the small print......

Whether it's your own development or your clients' development, it's essential to read all the documents and check out the small print. The only way you can be sure that you've got the right information is to check it out yourself. Even if you're paying a solicitor to sort out the contracts, you should read the documents yourself. If necessary, make a real nuisance of yourself by asking lots of questions of all your professional advisors, whether solicitors, accountants, VAT consultants(!), surveyors, architects and others about all aspects of the development, especially if it's your first property development, until you understand what it all means.

Chapter 3: Checklist

- You must get the basic facts correct on legal documents; e.g contracts.
- Use consistent references to avoid confusion.
- VAT reliefs for residential properties only apply if the finished properties will be USED for "qualifying" purposes.
- The VAT implications of any property transaction depend on the legal and commercial arrangements.
- There are many different types of joint venture arrangements and the VAT implications will depend entirely on the specific circumstances.
- Make sure you have proper planning permission, building consent etc, especially if things change after the work starts.
- The devil is in the detail, whether it's the VAT rules, planning permission or other legal documents. Make sure the facts are correct and that you understand the legal and commercial arrangements.

Chapter 4

What does "business" mean?

The business side of things: business and non-business properties

The word "business" is used a lot when we're discussing VAT and property. It can mean different things depending on the context and how it's used can affect the VAT liability of your development.

Here are the main situations when the term "business" is used in VAT:

- You may <u>be liable</u> to register or <u>be entitled</u> to register for VAT if your development is "in the course or furtherance of a business".
- The business <u>owner</u> is registered for VAT, not separate property developments or other business activities.
- There are different VAT rules for business (commercial) and non-business (residential) "qualifying" properties.
- Property developers claim VAT on their VAT returns. Non-business developers may be eligible to claim VAT under the DIY refund scheme.

HMRC guidance:

VAT Notice 700: The VAT Guide: section 3.1: Business transactions http://tinyurl.com/otpp58w
VAT Notice 700: section 4.6: Business/non-business http://tinyurl.com/ot5glbq
VAT Notice 700/1: Should I be registered for VAT: Who can register for VAT
http://tinyurl.com/q6ot9vn
VAT Notice 708: section 3.1.1: Qualifying properties: http://tinyurl.com/kenehzx.

"In the course or furtherance of a business"

VAT is a tax on the sale of goods or services " made in the course or furtherance of a business". HMRC explain the principles in detail in VAT Notice 700: The VAT Guide: section 3.1: **http://tinyurl.com/otpp58w**. It's worth taking a few minutes reading their guidance, especially if this is your first business venture.

The definition includes a wide range of activities, but for the purposes of this book, it's easier to explain what isn't regarded "in the course or furtherance of a business":

 "Non-business" includes: charitable use, free gifts of goods or services; personal use of goods and services.

> ### DIY builders and converters
>
> If you're *building or converting a property into a dwelling for your personal or family use*, then you can't register for VAT because your conversion is *not for a business purpose*. You may, however, be entitled to claim VAT on costs through the DIY VAT refund scheme.

The business owner is registered for VAT

As explained in Chapter 1, it's the owner of the business who registers for VAT. This also means that *every business activity of the VAT registered person is covered by the registration.* The business owner – be it a sole proprietor, limited company, partnership etc – must pay VAT on all income even if the income from each separate activity is below the VAT registration limit.

For example, suppose you register for VAT as a sole proprietor because you've converted an old commercial property into a dwelling and you're selling the freehold on completion. The sale qualifies as a zero-rated supply (as explained in Chapter 8) so you want to claim VAT on your costs.

However you also carry out construction services as a contractor for other people. The VAT registration also covers this activity so you'd also have to pay VAT on income from your construction services to HMRC.

See Chapter 17 for more information about VAT registration.

Different VAT rules for residential and commercial properties

The VAT reliefs explained in this book only apply to residential properties as explained in Chapter 2. They are defined as "qualifying properties" in VAT Notice 708: section 3.1.1: Qualifying properties: http://tinyurl.com/kenehzx. These include dwellings and certain properties used for relevant residential and relevant charitable purposes as defined in Appendix Two.

Commercial properties don't qualify for these reliefs. However there is a procedure called the "option to tax" which allows owners of certain non-residential properties to opt to charge VAT on their rental or sales proceeds. This also means that they can claim VAT on their expenditure.

The sale of new commercial properties and certain other limited types of income from commercial properties is liable to the standard rate of VAT.

I've summarized the main VAT rules for residential and commercial property in Chapter 5.

NB: Probably the only type of property that is subject to both residential and commercial rules are dwellings which are used for holiday lets. I've explained how the rules work for these properties in Chapter 9.

Business activities involving non-business properties

This is how it works:

- If you're building or converting or refurbishing "qualifying properties"; i.e. residential property, including dwellings, for sale, this is a business activity.
- Owning residential property and leasing the properties to generate income is a business activity.
- Building or converting any property to create dwellings for personal use, family use, or as a holiday home for personal/family is not a business activity.

How to benefit from VAT reliefs whether you're a business or non-business developer

---

VAT reliefs for residential properties

Both commercial and DIY developers can benefit from VAT reliefs on expenditure:

- If you're buying opted commercial properties to use as or convert to residential VAT free, you can issue certificate VAT 1614D to purchase the property VAT exempt. See Chapter 10.
- You can ensure contractors apply the zero-rate or reduced rate wherever possible for new construction, conversion or renovations. See Chapters 11 and 12.

However you claim VAT from HMRC under different procedures:

- Business developers: where eligible, recover VAT on conversion expenditure on VAT return as explained in Chapters 17 to 20.
- Non-business developers: where eligible, recover VAT on conversion expenditure through the VAT DIY House Converters Scheme.

Chapter 4: Checklist

- You can only register for VAT if you're carrying out taxable business activities, as explained in HMRC's VAT Notice 700.
- VAT registered businesses can't claim VAT on expenditure relating to their non-business activities.
- The VAT registration covers all the activities of the business owner.
- Business and non-business developers can benefit from the VAT reliefs on construction services and buying commercial properties VAT exempt to use or convert for residential purposes
- Non-business developers can't register for VAT but may be eligible to claim VAT on costs under the DIY refund scheme.

Chapter 5

Planning the development

VAT planning for property developments is important because VAT is a transaction tax and affects every single payment, whether made or received, for any business transaction. This means that you have to budget for VAT payments throughout the course of any property development.

And there are 3 specific other aspects that have to be taken into account:

- You have to be certain that you have <u>enough cash to pay any VAT on expenditure during the course of the project and avoid cash-flow problems caused by VAT refund delays</u>. Even if you can claim some or all of the VAT on your costs from HMRC on your VAT return, you have to PAY the VAT to your suppliers as you go along, so you have to budget for both the net cost and the VAT from the beginning.
- You also need to know <u>how much VAT you can claim</u> to work out the <u>VAT cost</u> of the development.
- And remember that <u>you can only claim VAT that has been correctly charged.</u>

That's why you need to factor VAT into the project planning process right from the start. It also means that developers have to understand how VAT applies to construction services to make sure that the contractors charge the zero-rate or reduced rate wherever possible.

Where to start?

Whenever I'm working with a property developer I find it helpful to develop a VAT "profile" to help me understand the commercial arrangements and identify the VAT issues. I usually do this in diagrammatic form, for example using a template like the one shown on the next page.

The planning permission

However you decide to deal with VAT, the first thing you need to know is what you're planning to do with the finished property. This is essential because you can ONLY benefit from the VAT reliefs for residential property if the property meets certain specific criteria, for example whether it has planning permission for residential purposes.

What next? The next stage is all about the contractual arrangements; i.e. "who is doing what for whom". That's when I find it useful to use a template and make sure that I have all the details of the developer's contractors, professional advisors and any other parties involved the development.

Of course, your own arrangements might look slightly different to the template. For example, if you're a developer, you might employ a single contractor to provide a "design and build" service, in which case all of the suppliers would provide their services to the main contractor, who would bill you for a single supply of construction services.

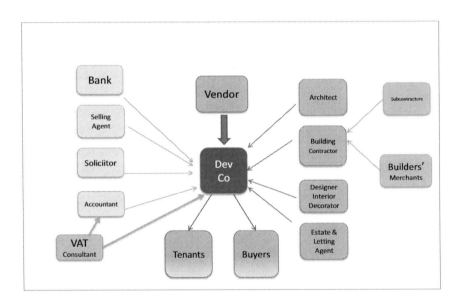

How do I work out the VAT cost?

As I explained in the Introduction, there are 3 stages to work out the VAT cost:

1. Start by confirming the VAT liability of the sales or rental income, from Chapters 7, 8 and 9.
2. Then look at Chapters 10 - 16 to find out how much VAT you can save on property and construction services.
3. Finally, check out the rules about claiming VAT on costs in Chapter 17 - 20.

Remember that you can't claim VAT that has been incorrectly charged by the contractor or supplier. So if the contractor charges 20% for work that was eligible for 5%, you have to ask the contractor to issue a credit note for the original invoice and a new invoice showing the correct VAT rate.

Chapter 5: Checklist

- Remember that all aspects of a development are linked for VAT purposes.
- VAT is a transaction tax so you need to factor the VAT into your budgeting to take account of paying contractors and when you can claim VAT from HMRC.
- Understanding the "big picture" contractual arrangements helps to establish the transactions for VAT purposes.
- You cannot claim VAT that is incorrectly charged, so make sure contractors charge the correct rate.

Chapter 6

Property and construction contracts

In this chapter, we'll look at contracts and VAT and the various issues that can arise.

- VAT and contracts
- Just because it's written down doesn't mean it's right!
- What if a contract is silent about VAT?
- Property transactions
  - Buying opted commercial properties
  - Tenanted properties
- Construction contracts
  - Pricing
- VAT inclusive or VAT exclusive?
- VAT related disputes
- Stamp duty land tax
- Other legal documents

VAT and contracts

Contracts contain the legal definition of the transaction so their content is important for VAT purposes.

It's essential that the contract explains the transaction correctly to avoid any disputes about the VAT liability. In this chapter, I've suggested how you might deal with certain VAT issues, but make sure that you discuss things with your solicitor.

VAT and contracts

I am not a solicitor and not qualified to give legal advice, so you should always rely on your solicitor's guidance when it comes to the form and content of any legal document. Many solicitors have a lot of experience when dealing with VAT and property issues and will be used to dealing with the subjects I've discussed in this chapter; others less so.

Some practical VAT problems can be avoided or minimized if the issues are dealt with in the contract. In this chapter, I've explained some of the most important so that you can ask your solicitor for advice about whether and how they can be covered in the contract.

The most important thing is that both parties agree on the VAT liability of the transaction, whether it's a property sale, lease or construction project and that the liability is defined in the contract.

You also should ensure that you're protected from unexpected VAT liability or related expenditure, such as interest or penalties, because of errors caused by the other party.

Just because it's written down doesn't mean it's right!

Nowadays, VAT officers almost always ask to see contracts and other legal documentation to make sure that the VAT treatment of the transaction is correct.

So make sure that the facts are correct. It's up to you to ensure your solicitor has the right information and review draft documents during the negotiation process to ensure that the documents reflect the transaction as you understand it. Ask your solicitor to explain or change something you don't understand or if you think it needs to be amended.

Solicitors often use pro-forma documents and amend them as required for different transactions. This sometimes means that relevant VAT issues are overlooked or, in some cases, may even be wrong or not apply. Remember, just because it's written down doesn't mean it's right so make sure you review documents properly.

What if a contract is silent about VAT?

For VAT purposes, the normal rule is that the value of ANY supply of goods or services, including the sale or lease or construction services for VAT purposes is the total amount payable in cash and the payment is treated as VAT inclusive. However contracts normally specific that the price of any goods or services is exclusive of VAT.

If the contract doesn't make it clear whether the price is VAT exclusive or VAT inclusive, the vendor/contractor may have to treat the amount charged as VAT inclusive. This means that the vendor/contractor's income is reduced by the VAT which reduces their profit, unless the customer is willing to pay VAT in addition to the agreed price.

So it's important that the contract stipulates whether the value is VAT inclusive or VAT exclusive to avoid disputes when the invoices are issued or payments made. Otherwise the contractor may have to pay any additional VAT out of his own pocket I've explained how to calculate VAT on VAT inclusive amounts and shown how much contractors can be out of pocket in the appendix to this chapter.

6.6   Property transactions

There are two types of property transaction which require special VAT actions by the purchaser to avoid VAT liabilities.

These are:

- Buying or selling opted commercial properties to use as or convert to residential use.
- Buying or selling property rental businesses.

In both of these transactions, *the VAT liability of the transaction depends on the purchaser carrying out certain actions within specific time limits.* It's particularly important that these issues are covered properly in the contracts, as explained below.

Buying opted commercial properties to convert to residential

If you're buying opted commercial properties to use as or convert to residential purposes, you can issue a certificate (VAT 1614D) to instruct the vendor to sell the property exempt from VAT. The law says that this has to be issued at a very specific time:

The certificate must be given before the price for the grant to the recipient by the seller is legally fixed, for example by exchange of contracts, letters or missives, or the signing of heads of agreement.

You can issue the certificate even if you subsequently decide not to purchase the property.

IT'S TOO LATE TO DO ANYTHING ONCE THE DEAL IS COMPLETED.

So as soon as you see a property that you may be interested in buying, I'd recommend issuing the certificate. The vendor may want to charge a higher price if the sale is exempt from VAT so you may need to do some further negotiating about the price.

Why deal with this issue in the contract when the certificate has already been issued?

Even though the certificate is issued BEFORE completion or exchange of contracts, the contract should include procedures in case there are any problems with the certificate, for example, how the parties should proceed if HMRC dispute the validity of the certificate.

The contract could also include provisions to determine which party is liable to pay any additional VAT; whether to dispute HMRC's ruling; how to deal with expenditure arising from the use of the certificate. See "Dealing with disputes" below.

The technical and practical issues of using the VAT 1614 procedure are explained in Chapter 10.

Tenanted properties

The sale of properties with existing tenants is normally regarded as the sale of a business as a going concern ("TOGC") and not the sale of the property. TOGCs aren't "supplies" for VAT purposes and they are subject to special rules that must be met by both buyer and seller.

The sale of a property rental business is a TOGC if certain conditions are met. There are additional specific rules about the sale of a commercial or mixed property rental business where the vendor has opted to tax the property OR if the property is a "new" commercial property. The purchaser is required to make his own option to tax the property and must notify the vendor and HMRC before the transaction is completed and in certain circumstances before any deposit is paid to the vendor or the vendor's agent.

It's therefore important that contracts for TOGC's include clauses for dealing with VAT on such transactions and include procedures to deal with situations where things go wrong.

The subject is covered in some detail in HMRC's Notice 700/9: Transfer of business as a going concern **http://tinyurl.com/m65xamv.** Sections 2 and 6 of the Notice deal specifically with property rental sales and related issues such as anti-avoidance and making any necessary adjustments on VAT returns.

Construction contracts

Our other area of interest is VAT on construction contracts. There are a number of specific VAT issues that cause problems in construction contracts, including VAT liability, payments and invoicing, as well as specific construction industry practices.

The VAT liability of construction work is one of the most common subjects for the Tax Tribunals and that's why it's important to agree the liability as soon as possible in the process and include clauses in the contract for dealing with disputes when the parties disagree.

It's a difficult area, as you'll see when you get to Chapters 11 and 12. So if possible, agree the VAT liability of the construction services before signing the contract, identifying any work that qualifies for the zero-rated or reduced rated.

There are links to VAT Notice 708; Buildings and construction for information about payment and invoicing issues for construction throughout the book.

Pricing: VAT inclusive or VAT exclusive?

Usually, the amount shown in a contract is the VAT exclusive value and the customer has to pay VAT on top of that amount. However, regardless of what the contract says, the seller has to pay any VAT due to HMRC <u>on the amount received from the customer,</u> whether or not VAT has been added to the price.

I've shown how this can affect a contractor's income in the appendix to this chapter.

Also, if the contractor issued a VAT invoice showing the net amount plus VAT, he has to pay the actual amount of VAT shown to HMRC <u>even if the purchaser refuses to pay the full amount of VAT</u>. His liability is still based on the VAT exclusive VAT, not the VAT inclusive price*.

Stamp duty land tax

If you sell a property which is liable to VAT, i.e. new commercial properties and opted commercial properties and the transaction is also subject to stamp duty land tax, VAT is charged on the total value of the property AND the stamp duty. See VAT Notice 742, section 7.10 http://tinyurl.com/bswtrlp.

Other issues and other legal documents

Sometimes, the main contract is quite short, but accompanied by several supporting documents such as schedules dealing with specific issues or containing details of assets.

There will also be property transfer forms and other regulatory documents, depending on the circumstances.

It's important to review legal documents yourself because it's your liability if there are any problems.

Chapter 6: Checklist

- The contract is the legal basis for any transaction. The VAT liability is based on the facts given in the contract.
- Your solicitor will advise you on the content and form of any contract, but ask if you don't understand anything.
- Make sure that the facts are correct – your solicitor will include information based on your instructions so check all of the details.
- Agree the VAT liability of the transaction in the contract and include procedures to deal with VAT related problems.
- Contracts for the purchase of opted commercial property for residential use or conversion and the purchase of property rental businesses may require additional clauses to deal with the special VAT issues.
- Read all contracts and other documentation carefully. It could be your liability if something goes wrong.

Chapter 6: Appendix

VAT inclusive/exclusive example

Extract from "VAT for DIY residential property developers"

What if the contractor charges 5% but HMRC say it should be 20%? If my contractor has to pay the difference to HMRC, how much does this cost?

If HMRC don't agree with the 5% or zero-rate, it could cost the contractor a significant amount of money.

Let's look at some figures

Take our contractor and suppose he has a contract that he has costed at £5,000 net of VAT. The difference between VAT at 5% and VAT at 20% is quite significant:

- o   £5,000 x 5% = £250.
- o   £5,000 x 20% = £1,000

The difference of £750 is a significant amount of money on this size of job.

Now, let's suppose that our contractor charges 5% VAT so the total bill is £5,250. HMRC reviews the return and tells the contractor that the job was liable to 20% VAT. The customer refuses to pay the additional £750.

This is where the calculations become a bit confusing. HMRC treat the £5250 as VAT inclusive, so to calculate 20% VAT included, they apply the "VAT fraction" and calculate the VAT as follows:

£5,250 x1/6 = £875.

The contractor paid £250 on his original VAT return, so he has to pay the difference:

£875 – £250 = £625

The £625 comes straight out of the contractor's pocket and probably means he loses money on the job.

It's easy to understand why contractors are careful about charging the reduced VAT rate of 5% or zero-rate.

Chapter 7

VAT and property rules

This chapter summarises the main VAT rules relating to residential and commercial property transactions and the VAT liability of construction work.

Construction services

- The construction of new residential properties is zero-rated. See Chapter 11.
- Construction services to change the number of dwellings in a property may qualify for the reduced rated. See Chapter 12.
- The conversion of non-residential properties to residential use may qualify for reduced rated conversion services. See Chapter 12.
- Renovations of dwellings that have been empty for at least two years are normally reduced rated. See Chapter 12.
- There are limited additional VAT reliefs for alterations to residential properties for the elderly and disabled. See Chapter 16.
- The installation of certain energy saving materials and grant funded heating systems are reduced rated. See Chapter 16.
- Other construction services, including work on residential property and ALL work on non-residential property, is standard rated.

Residential property sales and leases

- The first freehold or long leasehold sale by the "person constructing" qualifying residential properties (i.e. usually the developer) is zero-rated subject to certain conditions. See Chapter 8.
- The first freehold or long leasehold sale of a "non-residential conversion" by the "person converting" (i.e. usually the developer) is zero-rated subject to certain conditions. See Chapter 8.
- The first freehold or long leasehold sale of a substantially reconstructed listed/protected qualifying residential property by the "person reconstructing" qualifying residential properties (i.e. usually the developer) is zero-rated subject to certain conditions. See Chapter 8.
- Holiday lets are standard rated. See Chapter 9.
- Income from other residential properties, including residential lettings, is exempt from VAT

- If the owner of a commercial property has opted to tax the property, the purchase may be VAT exempt if the purchaser intends to use the property as a dwelling or issues a VAT 1614D certificate confirming that the property will be converted into a dwelling(s). See Chapter 10.

Commercial properties

- Any work on commercial property or civil engineering work, whether new construction, alteration, extensions or repairs, is liable to VAT at 20%.
- The sale of a new commercial property (up to 3 years old from the date of completion) is liable to VAT at 20%.
- Subsequent sales and other income from commercial property are exempt from VAT.
- Certain commercial property income is "excluded from exemption".
- However commercial property owners can "opt to tax" their properties which means that they charge VAT on sales and rental income and can claim VAT on expenditure.

See VAT Notices 742: Land and property: http://tinyurl.com/prw2zbm and 742a: Opting to tax land and buildings: http://tinyurl.com/plsxqmc for more information about commercial land and property transactions

Chapter 7: Appendix

VAT on common property developments

Residential property development: Quick guide

In this section I've listed some of the most common types of residential property developments; i.e. constructions, conversions, renovations of dwellings. For each, there is a summary of the VAT liability of income, VAT on the expenditure and when you can claim VAT from HMRC. It will also tell you which chapters you need to read for more detailed information about each issue.

Before you can work out the VAT cost, you need certain information, including:

- What sort of property are you building, converting, or refurbishing?
- Will it qualify as a residential property (see Chapters 2 and 7)
- If converting, what was the original property before conversion and what was it used for?
- Will the conversion change the number of dwellings in the property?
- How will the finished property be used?
- Will you be selling or leasing the finished property?
- If you're planning to lease the property, how long will the leases be?

Once you have this information, you can check the relevant section below for a summary of the main VAT issues.

1.   New build for sale

- Construction services by contractors can be zero-rated: see Chapter 11.
- Sale of freehold or grant of a long lease by the developer may qualify for zero-rating: see Chapter 8.
- Developer can claim VAT on expenditure under normal VAT rules: see Chapters 17 - 20.

2.   New build for leasing

- Construction services by contractors can be zero-rated: see Chapter 11.
- Short term residential lets are exempt from VAT: see Chapter 7.
- Developer can only claim VAT on expenditure if it is within the partial exemption "de minimis" limits: see Chapter 18.

3. Conversion of residential property for leasing

- Property purchase VAT exempt: see Chapter 7.
- Conversion services to change the number of dwellings or to a different residential purpose may qualify for the reduced rate: see Chapter 8.
- Short term residential lets are exempt from VAT: see Chapter 7.
- Developer can only claim VAT on expenditure if it is within the partial exemption "de minimis" limits: see Chapter 18.

5. Renovation of residential property for sale

- Property purchase VAT exempt: see Chapter 7.
- Renovation may qualify for the reduced rate: see Chapter 8.
- Sales of refurbished residential properties are exempt from VAT: See Chapter 7.
- Developer can only claim VAT on expenditure if it is within the partial exemption "de minimis" limits: see Chapter 18.
-

6. Renovation of residential property for leasing

- Property purchase VAT exempt: see Chapter 7.
- Renovation may qualify for the reduced rate: see Chapter 8.
- Short term residential lets are exempt from VAT: see Chapter 7.
- Developer can only claim VAT on expenditure if it is within the partial exemption "de minimis" limits: see Chapter 18.

7. Conversion of non-residential property for sale

- Property purchase normally VAT exempt: see Chapter 7.
- If vendor has opted to tax the property, the developer can purchase the property VAT exempt using VAT 1614D procedure: see Chapter 10.
- Conversion services may qualify for the reduced rate: see Chapter 12.
- First freehold sale by the developer may qualify for zero-rating: see Chapter 8.
- Developer can claim VAT on expenditure under the normal VAT claim rules. See Chapters 17 - 20.

8. Conversion of non-residential property for leasing

- Property purchase normally VAT exempt: see Chapter 7.
- If vendor has opted to tax the property, the developer can purchase the property VAT exempt using VAT 1614D procedure: see Chapter 10.
- Conversion services may qualify for the reduced rate: see Chapter 12.
- First grant of a long lease by the developer may qualify for zero-rating: see Chapter 8.
- However normal residential lets are VAT exempt; see Chapter 7.
- Developer cannot claim VAT on expenditure unless the VAT is within the partial exemption "de minimis" limits: see Chapters 17 - 20.

Some or all of the above

VAT issues can be particularly complicated if you're involved with any mixed developments, especially if your development is part residential and part commercial. First, you have to consider the VAT issues of each individual part, whether residential or commercial. Then you have to deal with apportionment for income and expenditure that doesn't relate to any specific property. This includes the following:

- If the vendor has opted to tax the property, you can use only use the VAT1614D procedure for that part of the property that you intend to use/convert for residential purposes.
- Construction work for residential parts of the development may qualify for the zero-rate or the reduced rate, while any work done on the commercial part will be standard rated.
- To benefit from the VAT savings on residential construction work, any work done to the common areas of the property must be apportioned. The contractor can charge the zero-rate/reduced rate on the part relating to the residential property. If the cost isn't apportioned the contractor has to charge VAT at the standard rate on the total value.
- If you sell or lease a building which incorporates different types of property, you might have to apportion your sales price or rent between the zero-rate, the standard rate and/or exempt.
- You may have to apply partial exemption rules to calculate how much VAT you can claim, including an apportionment method for VAT on expenditure that isn't directly attributable to specific parts of the property. You can only claim VAT on expenditure relating to exempt income if it is within the partial exemption "de minimis" limits.

New build or conversion for dwelling for personal use

If you're buying or converting for personal or family use, then you may be able to save VAT on new construction and conversion services as explained in Chapters 11 and 12. You may also be able to claim VAT on some of your costs under the VAT DIY Refund scheme. You can find information and claim forms here http://tinyurl.com/hhwmfex on HMRC's website.

Make sure that you read the information about the DIY Refund Schemes to find out what sort of DIY development qualifies for a refund before you spend any money. You don't want to incur costs only to find out that your development doesn't meet all of the necessary criteria.

You may also find my recent book "VAT for DIY residential property developers" helpful.

Case study: Introduction

The case study is a typical example of a developer who converts an old pub and builds some new houses on adjoining land. I've dealt with clients doing similar developments many times.

It's set out in 3 sections showing the 3 step process based on income from completed properties; VAT on expenditure and how much VAT the developer can claim from HMRC:

- VAT liability of income from the sale and lease of new and converted dwellings.
- VAT liability of expenditure, including construction services. This is the longest section and is in 2 parts to show the savings from the various VAT reliefs:
  - Calculates the worst case scenario; i.e. how much VAT would be payable if everything was liable to VAT at 20%.
  - Calculates how much VAT is payable with VAT savings.
- Shows how much VAT the developer can claim from HMRC.

The final VAT cost of the development is the difference between the VAT on expenditure and the VAT claimed from HMRC.

As you'll see, the case study is a somewhat simplified version of real life. For example, everything happens within a single VAT year, whereas in real life income and costs can be spread over several years. Also, certain issues are a lot less complicated than in real life - for example, apportioning the VAT cost of remedial work done to the roof and foundations of the property. I haven't shown this here because it would simply add unnecessary detail when the important thing is to show you how the process works in practice.

Either way, I'll refer back to the case study in future chapters of the book so that you can see how the theory of the VAT rules works in practice. It is only for illustration purposes, but not so far from many real life client situations.

But the most important thing is that by following the process through and understanding how the rules work, you can see *how the developer benefits from a worst case scenario where the VAT cost could be over £130,000 to calculating the potential final VAT cost of £15,200.*

However, I've also seen many situations where developers have assumed that they can benefit from VAT savings only to find out half way through the project that their development DOESN'T qualify and then had to find another £100,000, £120,000 or more to fund the unexpected VAT bill. *If you work out the VAT cost in advance and find that you CAN'T save VAT on costs or claim VAT from HMRC, at least you can budget for the additional cost so that it doesn't take away all of your anticipated profits.*

Apportionment

Apportionment of VAT on cost of work on common areas; i.e. work to roof & foundations

*Based on apportionment of proportion of the original property used for each conversion, the VAT cost can be allocated as follows:

House: £2,000 x 40% = £800.

Apartments: £2,000 x 60% = £1,200/2 = £600 per apartment.

**The VAT liability of this work could be further apportioned between the reduced rate and the standard rate, e.g. by reference to the value of standard rated/reduced rated goods and services in each converted dwelling. Not done for the purposes of this case study.

FACTS

The developer buys an old pub for conversion to flats and a house; with land for construction of 2 new houses on some vacant adjoining land.

The pub cost £160,000.

The building land cost £40,000.

The developer has planning permission for the work.

The developer plans to sell the converted house and new houses (freehold sales) and to lease the converted apartments on short term leases as investment properties. The existing pub does not include any self-contained dwelling nor was it used as a dwelling at any time.

The conversions will qualify as "non-residential conversions" (see Chapter 8).

40% of the existing pub property will be converted into the house, the remaining 60% shared equally for the 2 apartments.

All costs are incurred during the partial exemption year 1 April 2016 to 31 March 2017.

Step 1: VAT liability of income

The VAT liability of the income from the completed properties is based on how the properties will be used; i.e. freehold sale, grant of a long lease, short term residential leases. See Chapter 8 for the detailed rules. The zero-rate for the freehold sale and long lease will only apply if ALL of the criteria explained in Chapter 8 and HMRC VAT Notice 708, sections 4 and 5 are met.

- Freehold sale of new houses: zero-rated.
- Long lease of converted house (non-residential conversion): zero-rated.
- Short term residential lets of converted flats: exempt.

Step 2: VAT on costs.

Potential worst case scenario if all expenditure is liable to VAT at 20%.

Public house and grounds: £160,000. The vendor has opted to tax.

House conversion

- Property purchase: £32,000 x 40%* = £12,800
- House conversion: £75,000; Potential VAT cost: £15,000
- Additional goods and services that are not building materials; including free standing stove for the house; integrated appliances, "elaborate" vanity units for all 3 properties: £18,000.
  - House: £10,000. Potential VAT cost: £2,000
- Remedial work to the roof, foundations: Allocated to house: £4,000. Potential VAT cost: £800.*
- Re-surfacing car park to provide car parking spaces for each the converted house and apartments: £6,000; 2 for the house, 1 for each apartment. Potential VAT cost: £600
- Professional costs; including architects, surveyors, legal fees, and agents' fees: Converted house: £15,000 + VAT @20%: £3,000

Total potential VAT cost: £33,800

Apartments (per apartment)

- Property purchase: £32,000 x 60%* x 50% = £9,600
- Conversion costs: £50,000 each. Potential VAT cost: £10,000..
- Additional goods and services that are not building materials; including integrated appliances, "elaborate" vanity units for all 3 properties. Each apartment: £5,000 . Potential VAT per apartment: £1,000.
- Remedial work to the roof, foundations: Per apartment apportioned £3,000: Potential VAT cost: £600.*
- Re-surfacing car park to provide car parking spaces for each the converted house and apartments: £6,000; 2 for the house, 1 for each apartment. Potential VAT cost: per apartment: £300
- Professional costs; including architects, surveyors, legal fees, and agents' fees: Apartments: £6,000 per apartment @ 20% = £1,200

Potential VAT cost per apartment: £22,700

Total potential VAT cost: 2 apartments: £45,400

New houses (per house)

- Land: £20,000 @20% VAT = £4,000
- Labour and "building materials" per house: £90,000. Potential VAT cost: £18,000
- Additional goods and services that are not building materials; including basic landscaping work to provide soil, integrated units including oven, cooker; "elaborate" vanity units; electric garage doors and security systems: £10,000 per house, including goods @ £6,000; labour @ £4,000
    - Total goods: £6,000. Potential VAT cost: £1,200
    - Total labour: £4,000. Potential VAT cost: £800
- Professional costs; including architects, surveyors, legal fees, and agents' fees: £8,000 per house @ 20% = £1,600

Potential VAT cost per house: £25,600

Total potential VAT cost: 2 new houses: £51,200

Worst case scenario: total potential VAT cost for the whole development:

Converted house: £33,800

2 apartments: £45,400

2 new houses: £51,200

TOTAL :   **£130,400**

VAT costs WITH SAVINGS from zero-rate, reduced rate and exempt property purchase

Converted house

- VAT on property purchase: £32,000 x 40%* = £12,800. VAT 1614D procedure can be used to purchase property VAT exempt.   See Chapter 10.   VAT cost: NIL
- Conversion: £15,000. Qualifies for reduced rated conversion services. See Chapter 12.   VAT cost: £3,750
- Additional goods and services: £1,600. Reduced rate may apply to some services. See Chapter 15.   VAT cost: £1,600
- Remedial work: £800** Some reduced rating may apply. See notes.   VAT cost: £800
- Car parking spaces: £600. Reduced rate does not apply. See Chapter 12.   VAT cost: £600
- Professional fees etc: £3,000. Professional services standard rated.   VAT cost: £3,000

Total VAT cost with savings: £9,750

Each converted apartment

- Property purchase: £32,000 x 60%* x50% = £9,600. VAT 1614D procedure to purchase property VAT exempt. See Chapter 10.   VAT cost: NIL
- Conversion: £10,000.   Qualifies for reduced rated conversion services. See Chapter 12.   VAT cost: £2,500
- Additional goods and services: £1,000. Reduced rate may apply to some services. See Chapter 15.   VAT cost: £1,000
- Remedial work: £600**. Some reduced rating may apply. See notes.   VAT cost: £600
- Car parking spaces: £300. Reduced rate does not apply. See Chapter 12.   VAT cost: £300
- Professional fees etc: £1,200. Professional services standard rated.   VAT cost: £1,200

Total VAT cost with savings: £5,600

Each new house

- VAT on land: £4,000. VAT 1614D procedure does not apply to land. See Chapter 10.   VAT cost: £4,000

- Conversion: £10,000.   Qualifies for zero-rated construction services. See Chapter 11.   VAT cost: NIL
- Additional goods and services: see chapter 15.
    - Goods: £1,200 standard rated.   VAT cost: £1,200
    - Services: £800 zero-rated installation in course of construction   VAT cost: NIL
- Remedial work: N/A.   VAT cost: NIL
- Car parking spaces: N/A   VAT cost: NIL
- Professional fees etc: £1,600. Professional services standard rated.   VAT cost: £1,600

Total VAT cost with savings £10,400

Total VAT cost WITH SAVINGS for the whole development:

Converted house: £9,750

2 apartments: £11,200

2 new houses: £20,800

        TOTAL :   **£41,750**

Step 3: Calculate how much VAT the developer can claim from HMRC?

Converted house

Claim VAT on all costs except "other goods"; i.e. non-business materials. See Chapter 15.

VAT on cost of converted house: £9,750

Less VAT cost of "other goods": £1,600

Total to claim: £8,150

Converted flats

No VAT can be claimed because the costs are all directly attributable to exempt supplies. See Chapter 17.

2 apartments: £11,200

New houses

Claim VAT on all costs except "other goods"; i.e. non-business materials. See Chapter 15.

VAT on expenditure of 2 new houses: £20,800

Less VAT cost: £1,200 x 2 = £2,400

Total to claim: £18,400

Final VAT cost

Converted house: £1,600

Converted flats: £11,200

New houses: £2,400

Final VAT cost: £15,200

The 3 step process: Stage 1

VAT on income

Chapter 8

Zero-rated sales of new residential properties, converted commercial buildings and listed buildings

> This chapter explains the 3 situations when business owners can register for VAT and claim VAT from HMRC on the expenditure of new residential properties, certain converted non-residential properties and certain listed buildings.

In this chapter, we'll be looking at some quite detailed, technical rules about selling residential property. However they are important because **your property sales only qualify for zero-rating if each and every one of the relevant conditions is fully met.**

It is a long chapter because I've explained in some detail how the rules apply to each type of zero-rated sale; i.e. new properties, converted properties and listed properties.

Why is zero-rating important?

- Zero-rated sales and leases: VAT registration
- Other residential sales and lettings

Extract from VAT Act 1994, Schedule 8, Group 5: The law for the zero-rate applies of sales of new and converted residential properties

Zero-rated sales

1. Zero-rating sales of new residential properties

- First grant
- Major interest
- Person constructing
- Qualifying buildings

2. Zero-rating sales of converted commercial properties

- First grant
- Major interest
- Person converting
- Non-residential conversion
- Does the zero-rate apply to the sale of all properties which qualified for reduced rated conversion work?
- Problem areas:
  - living accommodation which isn't self-contained
  - when "new" dwellings incorporate part of an existing dwelling

3. Substantially reconstructed listed buildings

- Withdrawal of zero-rating for alterations of listed buildings in 2012
- Conditions for zero-rating the sale of substantially reconstructed listed buildings

Other related issues

- Other issues
- Garages
- Sales of part completed properties
- Relevant residential properties: certificates

Please read this chapter in conjunction with VAT Notice 708, section 4: Zero-rating the sale of, or long lease, in new buildings http://tinyurl.com/q7ekzyk; section 5: Sales of converted non-residential properties http://tinyurl.com/pxjrjuz and section 10: sales of substantially reconstructed listed buildings http://tinyurl.com/m8u2pro.

N.B. Holiday accommodation: See Chapter 9 for further information about using dwellings for holiday lets.

Why is zero-rating important?

As explained in <u>Chapter 1</u>, there are two classes of supplies – or sales – for VAT purposes; taxable and exempt. Taxable sales include those at the standard rate of 20%, the reduced rate of 5% and the zero-rate. Exempt supplies aren't liable to VAT.

The other important difference between taxable and exempt is:

- Businesses making taxable sales at any rate – including zero rated supplies - <u>can claim VAT on goods and services used to make those supplies.</u>
- Businesses making exempt supplies <u>can't normally claim VAT</u> on goods and services used to make those supplies. This VAT is called "exempt input tax". The main exception to this rule is if the business's "exempt input tax" falls within certain "de minimis" limits, which are currently £625 per month and 50% of the business's total input tax on average.

This distinction is very important for property developers. Normal residential rental income is exempt from VAT, but the freehold sale or long lease of certain new residential properties and certain converted non-residential properties is zero-rated. This means that residential developers can normally only claim VAT on expenditure if they make zero-rated sales such as those discussed in this chapter.

When the zero-rate relief applies

Sales and rentals of residential property are normally exempt from VAT. However there are three exceptions to this which are discussed in this chapter.

1: Freehold sales and grants of long leases of new residential properties.

2: Freehold sales and grants of long leases of converted non-residential property.

3: Freehold sales and grants of long leases of substantially reconstructed protected residential properties.

Claiming VAT on expenditure can make an important contribution to the overall profitability of any development, so it's important to understand how these rules work in practice. The conditions for zero-rating the sales/long leases of these 3 types of property are explained below.

How do you claim VAT?

Zero-rated sales and leases: VAT registration

If you make taxable supplies, whether at the standard rate of 20%, the reduced rate of 5% or the zero-rate, you have to register for VAT to claim VAT on your costs.

You have to notify HMRC that you are liable to register for VAT when your taxable sales exceed the VAT registration limit, which is currently £85k per annum (May 2017). If the value of the property sale(s) and income from any other taxable business activity exceeds this limit, you must apply to register for VAT.

You can also register for VAT on a voluntary basis if your turnover is below the registration limit. In these situations, you would be able to claim VAT on expenditure relating to your zero-rated sale(s).

Chapter 17 explains how and when to register for VAT; and when you can register BEFORE making any sales so that you can claim VAT on costs during the course of a construction or conversion development.

Other residential sales and lettings

If your sale/lease doesn't qualify for the zero-rate or as a standard rated holiday let (see Chapter 9), then your income will be exempt from VAT. If this is your only income, then you can't register for VAT and you can't claim VAT on your costs.

If you make any other taxable supplies - e.g. you run an estate agency, generating taxable agency fees at 20%, and let a couple of your own properties generating exempt rent - then you can register for VAT and claim VAT on costs relating to the estate agency. You can also claim VAT related to your let properties if it falls within the "de minimis" limit (£625 per month and 50% of all input tax on average - see Chapter 1).

See Chapters 17 - 20 for more information about claiming VAT from HMRC.

The conditions for zero-rating the sale of residential properties

I've avoided quoting legislation or referencing the law in this book, but I've made an exception in this case because this particular extract is so important. This first extract zero-rates both the sale of new qualifying buildings (section (a))and the sale of converted non-residential buildings (section (b)). The second applies to sales of certain reconstructed listed buildings.

This law says that zero-rating applies to:

"The first grant by a person -

(a) constructing a building –
     (i)   designed as a dwelling or number of dwellings; or
     (ii) intended for use solely for a relevant residential or a relevant charitable purpose, or
(b) converting a non-residential building or a non-residential part of a building into a building designed as a dwelling or number of dwellings or a building intended for use solely for a relevant residential purpose,

of a major interest in, or in any part of, the building, dwelling or its site."

Extract from VAT Act 1994, Schedule 8, Group 5, Item 1.

For listed building the law says that zero-rating applies to:

"The first grant by a person substantially reconstructing a protected building, of a major interest in, or in any part of, the building or its site."

Extract from VAT Act 1994, Schedule 8, Group 6,, Item 1.

These extracts from the VAT Act provide the zero-rating for the sale of certain new, converted and reconstructed listed buildings. In each case, they include 4 particularly important criteria:

- first grant;
- major interest;
- person constructing/converting/reconstructing; and
- qualifying building.

Each of these criteria is explained below.

Zero-rated sales

1. New residential properties

Let's discuss each of these criteria in the context of new residential properties.

Condition 1: the first grant of a major interest.

What does this mean?

As explained in Chapter 2, a "grant" can include a freehold sale, or grant of a long lease in a property.

In this context, in order to be zero-rated, the grant must be the first grant of either the freehold sale or the grant of a long lease, as explained below in Condition 2.

A good example of the "first grant" principle would be a housebuilder who intended to sell some new dwellings but has to let them for a couple of years because he can't sell them. Eventually, he sells the freeholds. The freehold sales are zero-rated because they are the first grant of a major interest in the property, even though he has granted short term residential leases in the meantime.

Zero-rating only applies to the first premium or rental payments, so any future rental payments are exempt. For example, suppose you grant a zero-rated 999 year lease in a dwelling in return for an intial premium and annual ground rent. This means that you can claim VAT on expenditure related to the intial sale, but VAT on subsequent expenditure relating to the ongoing exempt rental income would be "exempt input tax". You can only claimed this VAT if it's within the "de minimis" limit.

Condition 2: "Major interest"

As explained in Chapter 2, a "major interest" is either the freehold sale or lease over 21 years. In Scotland it refers to either the estate or interest of the owner or the tenant's interest under a lease for a term of not less than 20 years. See VAT Notice 708, s5.2 http://tinyurl.com/pwesawt for more details.

Short term residential lets are defined as "minor interests" and are therefore exempt from VAT.

Condition 3: "Person constructing"

The second criteria is that the sale must be make by the "person constructing" the property. What does this mean?

It normally means the person who owns the property and has either carried out the construction themselves; or engaged contractors to carry out the construction work.   So it would typically be a property developer.

However, HMRC defines the "person constructing" as follows:

*"You are a 'person constructing' a building if, in relation to **that** building, you are acting as, or you have, at any point in the past, acted as:*

- *a **developer** – you physically constructed, or commissioned another person to physically construct, the building (in whole or in part) on land that you own or have an interest in; or*
- *a **contractor or subcontractor** - you provided construction services to the developer or another contractor for the construction of the building, sub-contracting work as necessary."*

VAT Notice 708, section 4.5.1 http://tinyurl.com/mjfm95e.

This means that more than one "person" can have "person constructing" status in relation to the same property. What does this mean in practice? A good example of this would be if a developer started work on a site with some new dwellings but went bankrupt before the site was finished and had to sell the site. He would be regarded as "person constructing", so the sale of the site would be zero-rated.

Suppose the site was purchased by a different developer, who completes the site and sells the individual houses. In this case, the second developer would also be regarded as "person constructing" so could zero-rate the sale of the houses.

Zero-rating can also apply to sales of, or long leases in partially constructed properties. VAT Notice 708, section 4.7: http://tinyurl.com/pkz3oskexplains how the rule applies to partially constructed properties.

Condition 4: Qualifying properties

New properties must be a "qualifying property" to qualify for zero-rated sales; i.e. a dwelling, or property used for "relevant residential purposes" or for "relevant charitable purposes" as defined in Chapter 2.

2. Converted commercial property; i.e. "non-residential conversions"

Now we'll consider how the rules apply to the sale of converted non-residential property.

The legislation shown earlier in this chapter also zero-rates the sale of converted non-residential property as for new properties, so some of the definitions will be the same.

N.B HMRC's main guidance about this subject is VAT Notice 708, section 5 http://tinyurl.com/ozqg4e4. It contains some very helpful guidance about the meaning of "conversion" and the types of property that can qualify. I've included several links in this section to help you find relevant information quickly.

Condition 1: the first grant of a major interest

This definition is the same as for new properties.

Condition 2: "Major interest"

The same as for new residential properties.

Condition 3: "person converting"

HMRC defines the term "person converting" as:

*"You are a 'person converting' a building if, in relation to **that** building, you are acting as, or have, at any point in the past, acted as:*

- *a **developer** - you physically converted, or commissioned another person to physically convert, a building (in whole or in part) that you own or have an interest in;*
- *a **contractor or subcontractor** - you provided construction services to the developer or another contractor for the conversion of the building, sub-contracting work as necessary."*

VAT Notice 708; s5.5.1: http://tinyurl.com/onf5lvj.

Like the "person constructing" criteria, this means that the "person converting" status can apply to more than one party.

An example of the "person converting" status applying to more than one person is as follows: a developer acquires the freehold of an old office block which he starts to convert into flats. With about 60% of the conversion work done, the developer goes bankrupt and sells the freehold of the partially completed property to help fund his debts.

The freehold is sold to the main building contractor who completes the conversions and sells 999 year leases in each of the new apartments.

In this example, both the developer and contractor have "person converting" status in respect of the property and are both entitled to zero-rate the sale of the freehold or long leases in the property, meaning that they can claim VAT on their expenditure.

Zero-rating can also apply to sales of, or long leases in partially constructed or converted properties. VAT Notice 708, section 5.7 http://tinyurl.com/prma4sm: explains how the rule applies to partially converted properties.

Condition 4: Converted non-residential buildings

This is probably the most important and most difficult criteria about the sale of converted properties.

To qualify for the zero-rate, the converted properties must be a "qualifying property"; i.e. either a dwelling or a "relevant residential" property as defined in Chapter 2.

HMRC uses the term "non-residential conversion". I've explained the main issues below.

"Non-residential conversions"

This definition applies in two situations:

- If you're converting a property that was not a dwelling, adapted as a dwelling or used as a dwelling: it must become a dwelling or number of dwellings or property used for "relevant residential purposes"after the conversion.

This means that the original property was used for commercial purposes, such as shop or a factory or an office block or a public house. It can also include commercial properties that contain some residential part such as staff accommodation as explained on the next page.

HMRC's main guidance about this subject is in VAT Notice 708, section 5.3 http://tinyurl.com/ozqg4e4.

The legal definitions of the terms "designed as a dwelling" and property used for "relevant residential purposes"are in Appendix 1 (Definition 1). It is important that your conversions meet all of the criteria included in the definition to qualify as a "non-residential conversion".

- Unoccupied dwellings: The other definition of "non-residential conversions" can also include existing dwellings in the following very limited circumstances: if a dwelling(s) or property used for "relevant residential purposes" was constructed more than ten years before the grant of the major interest; and no part of the building has, in the period of ten years immediately preceding the grant, been used as a dwelling or for a relevant residential purpose (the "ten year rule").

This means that the restoration of any existing dwelling that hasn't been occupied for ten years is a "non-residential conversion". Certain limited occupation can be "ignored" when considering the "ten year rule"; see VAT Notice 708 section 5.3.2 http://tinyurl.com/ozqg4e4.

In either case, the converted dwelling(s) must not become holiday accommodation. This means that there must not be any planning restrictions which include any restriction on year-round habitation or disposal. See Chapter 9 more information about holiday lets.

Does the zero-rate apply to freehold sales and long leases in all converted properties?

This is one of the most confusing subjects but it's extremely important, because it affects whether or not developers can claim VAT on conversion costs.

The answer is that the zero-rate only applies to the sale of additional dwellings or a property (or properties) used for "relevant residential purposes" created from existing non-residential properties.

HMRC give the following examples:

- "a commercial building (such as an office, warehouse, shop),
- an agricultural building (such as a barn), or
- a redundant school or church"

What does this mean? If you sell new dwellings that are created from converted dwellings, for example, by extending existing houses, or changing the number of apartments in an existing apartment block, their sale will be exempt because the conversion isn't a "non-residential conversion".

Problem areas

As I explained in Chapter 2, the term "conversion" can cause confusion because a different set of criteria apply for the purposes of the reduced rate on construction services and for the zero-rate. The criteria for reduced rate construction services are explained in Chapter 12.

I've explained the main situations when the sale of "converted" residential properties doesn't qualify for the zero-rate.

The zero-rate doesn't apply if you've converted a pub or office which has living accommodation, even if it isn't self-contained. This is because the conversion isn't regarded as a non-residential conversion because the property has previously been used as a dwelling; which usually means somebody's home. This also applies to crofts, bed-sit accommodation and similar multi-occupancy properties.

If the property has been adapted to use as a dwelling

The zero-rate won't apply if the property has been "adapted"; for example by installing a family bathroom or kitchen in the property.

What happens if the "new" dwelling incorporates part of an existing dwelling?

HMRC's view is that if an additional dwelling(s) is created by the conversion of a part of the building that was previously non-residential, zero-rating is limited to the grant in that part of the building only where the additional dwelling(s) is contained wholly within the non-residential part.

What does this mean in practice?

Suppose you buy a pub which has an existing flat on the top floor, in which the manager lived. There is space to create an additional flat as there are other rooms that were used for business; e.g. rooms let out for weddings, meetings etc.

So you have 2 options:

- You refurbish leave the existing flat and convert the remaining rooms to create an additional, self-contained flat. In this case, the sale of the refurbished flat is exempt and the sale of the new flat is zero-rated, so you can claim VAT on the conversion costs.
- You might want to change the layout of the existing flat so that some of the space is incorporated into the new flat. In this case, the sale of the smaller existing flat is exempt. The sale of the new flat is also exempt because it incorporates part of the existing residential property.

So you can see just how a simple thing such as the layout of a couple of flats can affect your profit because in one scenario you can claim VAT on the costs, in another you can't. And it doesn't matter whether the part of the existing dwelling incorporated is large or small.

In either case, remember that you can't claim VAT from HMRC that has been incorrectly charged, so it's important that your contractor charges reduced rated VAT for his services as far as possible. See Chapter 12 for information about the reduced rate for conversion work. And if you can't claim the VAT because the sales are exempt, then it's even more important that you take advantage of the reduced rate to keep your costs down.

This is a complicated area of the law so it's not surprising that there have been several disputes about conversions between HMRC and property developers over the years. There are many rulings from the VAT Tribunal and the courts about how the law applies in these situations, so if you're considering any sort of non-residential conversion that doesn't fit neatly into the rules as explained in HMRC's Notices, I'd strongly recommend that you consider carefully how the rules would apply in your situation and take professional advice if you're in any doubt.

I've included a short appendix to this chapter to show how the reduced rate for conversions/renovations and the zero-rate for sales of converted non-residential properties apply and how even small differences in the development can have a significant effect on the developer's costs. You might also want to come back to this appendix when you're reading Chapter 12 about the reduced rate.

3. Sales of substantially reconstructed listed (i.e. "protected") buildings

Zero-rating also applies to sales of substantially reconstructed listed residential buildings under similar provisions for new residential properties and non-residential conversions. This means that developers of such properties can register for VAT and claim VAT on related expenditure.

However, there is still a lot of confusion about VAT on alterations carried out on listed buildings. As explained below, the zero-rate no longer applies to such work.

> **Zero-rating for approved alterations to listed buildings was withdrawn with effect from 1 October 2012. At the same time, rules for zero-rating the sale of substantially reconstructed listed buildings were tightened.**

Under the old rules, the "first grant of a major interest by a person reconstructing" was zero-rated when 3/5ths of the cost of the work were approved alterations; or where the building was reconstructed from a shell.

From 1 October 2012, zero-rating was limited to *the first grant of a listed building made by the person who has substantially reconstructed the building from a shell*.

Transitional arrangements allow the zero-rating under the original rules to apply until 30 September 2015, but only if certain arrangements were in place on or before 20 March 2012. See VAT Notice 708, section 9: http://tinyurl.com/ktqldmf for more information about approved alterations and the transitional arrangements.

What is "substantially reconstructed"?

Following the 2012 Budget changes,the definition is now as follows:

"A protected building is substantially reconstructed when:

- *reconstruction takes place that is major work to the building's fabric, including the replacement of much of the internal or external structure; and*

- *the reconstruction involves 'gutting' the building – that is no more of the original building is retained than an external wall or walls, or external walls together with other external features of architectural or historic interest."*

What does this mean in practice?

If you sell a listed property which has been "substantially reconstructed", you can register for VAT and claim VAT on the reconstruction expenditure that are attributable to the zero-rated sale under the principles explained above.

VAT Notice 708, section 10: http://tinyurl.com/m8u2pro provides further information about the revised rules and transitional arrangements.

However, if you are converting a commercial listed building to residential use, then the conversion work may qualify for the reduced rate under the rules explained in Chapter 12. Also the sale of the converted property may qualify for the zero-rate if it falls within the rules as a "non-residential conversion" as explained in Part 2 of this chapter.

Other issues

Sales of new and converted residential properties: partly completed properties, apportionment, and other issues

Notice 708, sections 4 and 5 explain other issues about the zero-rating of new residential properties and converted non-residential properties, including beneficial property owners; sales by members of VAT groups; There is also other helpful guidance on issues such as apportionment and partly completed properties.

Please take the time to read the relevant sections in Notice 708 section 4: http://tinyurl.com/q7ekzyk about new buildings or section 5: http://tinyurl.com/pxjrjuz about converted non-residential buildings to make sure that you've considered all of the issues contained in HMRC's guidance.

Converted garages

If you sell a converted garage which has been occupied with a dwelling into an additional dwelling; or other buildings such as barns, the sale is VAT exempt, not zero-rated. Such conversions aren't "non-residential conversions" because the buildings were part of an existing dwelling. The creation of the additional dwelling may, however, qualify for reduced rated conversion services as explained in Chapter 12.

> **Definitions**
>
> Remember that there are 3 separate definitions of the word "dwelling" that apply in different circumstances.

However if you convert a garage that was never used to store vehicles, or hasn't been used to store vehicles for a long period of time, then the conversion may qualify as a "non-residential conversion".

See VAT Notice 708, s5.7 http://tinyurl.com/prma4sm for further information about converted garages and other out-buildings.

Relevant residential properties and relevant charitable properties

Certificates

If you sell a new property used for "relevant residential purposes"or "relevant charitable purposes" , the buyer must provide a certificate confirming that the property will be used for "relevant residential purposes"or "relevant charitable purposes" as appropriate.

Buyers must also provide a certificate if buying a non-residential property which has been converted into a property to be used for "relevant residential" purposes.

VAT Notice 708, section 17: http://tinyurl.com/otdbzte explains how and when certificates are required:. The certificate needed to claim zero-rating on the purchase of a property to be used for "relevant residential purposes"or "relevant charitable purposes"property is shown in Notice 708, section 18.2: http://tinyurl.com/lokgohg.

Chapter 8: Checklist

- Freehold sales and long leases of "non-residential property conversions" by the "person converting" are zero-rated.
- This means that the converter can register for VAT and recover VAT on the conversion expenditure.
- The relief only applies when specific conditions are met:
    - First grant
    - Major interest
    - Person constructing or converting
    - New residential property or "non-residential conversion".
- There are different criteria for zero-rated sales of "non-residential conversions" and reduced rated conversion work.
- Sales of major interests in substantially reconstructed listed conversions can also be zero-rated under similar rules.

Chapter 8: Appendix

Residential conversions and renovations

Explains when the reduced rate of conversions and renovation services and zero-rating for the sale of converted non-residential properties apply to typical residential developments.

I've set out below an examples showing how apparently similar developments can have very different VAT profiles.

Example

Facts: An old pub which ceased trading twelve months ago has a self-contained flat upstairs where the landlord and his family lived. This flat is refurbished and the developer grants a 99 year lease in the refurbished flat. The downstairs pub area is converted into a separate flat and a 99 year lease is sold.

The renovation of the upstairs flat is standard rated (no reduced rate because the property was occupied during the past two years). The conversion of the pub area is reduced rated as the creation of a new dwelling, see Chapter 12.

The sale of the lease in the refurbished flat is exempt, so the VAT on the costs is "exempt input tax".

The sale of the lease in the conversion is zero-rated as a non-residential conversion; see Chapter 8. The developer can register for VAT and claim the VAT paid on the conversion expenditure relating to that dwelling.

Because the sale of the existing flat is exempt, the developer can't claim the "exempt input tax" on the renovation expenditure unless it VAT is within the developer's partial exemption "de minimis" limit as explained in Chapters 17 - 20.

Facts: The property in the above example is converted into a single house and the freehold is sold.

The conversion work is standard rated as the number of dwellings in the property doesn't change.

The sale is exempt from VAT.

The sale is exempt so the developer can't claim VAT on the conversion expenditure unless the VAT is within his "de minimis" limit as explained in Chapters 17 - 20.

Facts: The pub and the apartment in Example 3 is converted into 2 semi-detached houses and each sold as a freehold sale.

The conversion work qualifies for reduced rating in respect of the work done to the first floor. Conversion work done to the ground floor is standard rated. See Chapter 13 where I've explained why different VAT rates apply in this situation.

The sale of the newly converted houses is exempt. The zero-rate doesn't apply because the conversions are not "non-residential conversions" because both houses contain part of the existing residential accommodation. See Chapter 8.

The developer can't claim VAT on the costs unless the VAT is within his partial exemption "de minimis" limit as explained in Chapters 17 - 20.

Chapter 9

Holiday accommodation

In this chapter, I'll discuss the VAT implications of letting a dwelling for holiday lettings.

Holiday accommodation can be provided in a variety of ways, including dwellings or in "commercial" property such as holiday parks, hotels, purpose built holiday homes, such as houses or apartments.

There is also a special VAT accounting scheme called the "Tour Operators Margin Scheme" ("TOMS") that applies if businesses sell holiday accommodation or other travel related services which I'll explain briefly in this chapter. Usually you only have to use this scheme if you're "reselling" such services; e.g. a package including travel and accommodation, to the final customer. It can also apply if you sell certain "bought-in" services to your customers along with your holiday let.

In either case, if your income from holiday lets and other "taxable" exceeds the VAT registration limit, you have to register for VAT and charge VAT on the income. Because the income is liable to VAT, you can claim VAT on related costs.

One of the main things that confuses people is the fact that holiday lets are sometimes as commercial property for VAT purposes, or as "dwellings" for VAT purpose. But, as I've explained in this chapter, the type of property doesn't matter - it's a "holiday let" if it's advertised for use as a holiday let.

- What is a holiday let?
- Dwellings used as holiday lets
- Income from holiday lets
- Tour Operators Margin Scheme
- VAT recovery and partial exemption
- Using your own home for holiday lets

What's a holiday let?

HMRC's guidance about holiday lets is VAT Notice 709/3: hotels and holiday accommodation, paragraph 5 http://tinyurl.com/znrxk2p.

It says" Accommodation advertised or held out as suitable for holiday or leisure use is always treated as holiday accommodation." It includes, "but is not restricted to, any house, flat, chalet, villa, beach hut, tent, caravan, or houseboat".

So if you advertise any dwelling (whether new or converted or existing properties) for holiday use, this is regarded as holiday accommodation for VAT purposes. This is regarded as a business activity so the income counts towards your VAT registration limit.

Dwellings used for holiday lets

How does this work for VAT purposes?

For VAT purposes, holiday lets can include letting one or more properties as holiday lets, or even just your own home for part of the year.

However, there are a number of differences for VAT purposes if property is purpose built rather than a dwelling.

Purpose built holiday accommodation; i.e. not a dwelling:

- New construction, conversions and renovations are liable to VAT at the standard rate.

- The freehold sale of "new" (3 years from date of completion) purpose built holiday accommodation are liable to VAT at the standard rate.

  - The standard rate also applies to the first sale or long lease of a new building (or part of building) designed as a dwelling if the building is a new building and the seller/grantee is

    o not entitled to reside in the accommodation throughout the year
    o prevented from residing in the accommodation throughout the year by the terms of a covenant, statutory planning permission or similar restriction, or
    o prevented from using the accommodation as his principle private residence by the terms of a covenant, statutory planning permission or similar restriction

    HMRC confirms that "In these circumstances, the supply is treated as a supply of 'holiday accommodation' even if the accommodation would not otherwise be regarded as holiday accommodation" because the property can't be used as a dwelling. See VAT Notice 709/3, paragraph 5.3 http://tinyurl.com/m9wotnr.

- If you sell property as part of the sale of a business as a going concern, then the sale may not be liable to VAT if it meets the criteria outlined in VAT Notice 700/9: Transfer of business as a going concern: http://tinyurl.com/pbwvq45.

- Rental income and service charges income from holiday lets are standard rated. See Notice 709/3, paragraph 5.4 http://tinyurl.com/kpoehpb.

If the property is a dwelling:

If your property is a "dwelling", then the VAT liability of the sale or rent from normal residential leases follows the normal rules explained in Chapter 7.

To qualify as a "dwelling", there should be no restriction on the property being a full time residence, whether by the local planning authority, or any other covenant or other legal provision relating to the property in question. These restrictions on use are explained in paragraph 5 of VAT Notice 709/3 http://tinyurl.com/kpoehpb. There should also be no restriction on the separate disposal of the property, as explained see the definition in Appendix 2.

What does this mean in practice?

- The construction, conversion or renovation may qualify for the zero-rate or reduced rate explained in Chapters 11 and 12.

- You may be entitled to claim VAT on new construction and certain conversions under the VAT DIY refund scheme.

- The sale of certain new dwellings and converted dwellings may qualify for the zero-rate as explained in Chapter 8. Otherwise the sale or rental income as a dwelling is VAT exempt.

Off season lettings

Whether or not your property qualifies as a dwelling or is strictly commercial property, off season lettings of more than 28 days*, including short term residential lets, are exempt from VAT. In this case, then the whole let is VAT exempt as long as the following criteria are met:

- it is let as residential accommodation
- it is let for more than 28 days, and
- holiday trade in the area is clearly seasonal

*See Notice 709/3, paragraph 5.6 http://tinyurl.com/kpoehpb which explains the circumstances when the letting can be VAT exempt in more detail.

Tour Operators Margin Scheme ("TOMS")

The TOMS is a scheme that normally applies to tour operators who sell package holidays, including accommodation, travel and other related services. However it can also apply to any business who sells related services even if it doesn't constitute a whole "package". For example, if you buy theatre tickets, or pay for transport for your guests, then in principle your business would fall within the TOMS.

Under the scheme, the business can't recover VAT on expenditure but only has to pay HMRC VAT on the profit element of the selling price. In principle you don't pay any more VAT than under normal VAT accounting, but you must do the calculations following the margin scheme method. It's explained in detail in VAT Notice 709/5: Tour operators margin scheme: http://tinyurl.com/2rbowd.

So if you're selling holiday accommodation using your own property for the holiday let along with other related services, you may be required to use this scheme. However there are some exclusions if income from certain TOMS "supplies" is very low, as explained in Notice 709/5, section 3.6 http://tinyurl.com/z3m69jq.

The TOMS is a particularly complicated area of VAT and I'd strongly recommend that you do your research and take advice if you're thinking of selling any other services in addition to holiday lets.

VAT registration and claiming VAT on costs

If your only income that is liable to VAT is from holiday lets, then you register for VAT in the same way as any other business, as explained in Chapter 17: Being a VAT registered business.

If you're registering for VAT for the first time, you claim the VAT on pre-registration costs under the normal pre-registration rules - see VAT Notice 700, paragraph 11 http://tinyurl.com/kk92jgg for the detailed rules - if the goods and services will be used to make taxable supplies after registration. But if ANY of the VAT incurred pre-registration relates to exempt supplies made after registration, then you cannot claim any of the pre-registration VAT relating to those exempt supplies.

So if your property/properties will be used for both taxable holiday lets and exempt residential lets, you can't claim VAT on ANY pre-registration costs that relate to the exempt supplies. Also as business is partly exempt and may not be able to claim all of the VAT on its costs once registered, as discussed below.

VAT on costs: partial exemption

Owners of holiday accommodation can recover VAT on expenditure relating to their taxable income, including running and maintenance expenditure, conversion or renovation work under the normal VAT rules. However if you also make exempt supplies, then you can only claim the VAT on related costs ("exempt input tax") if it falls within the "de minimis" limit as explained in Chapter 18. In this case, your business is "partly exempt".

One of the most important things about claiming VAT on costs is that you can only claim VAT that has been correctly charged by the supplier. If a building contractor charges 20% VAT for work that qualified for the reduced rate or zero-rate, then you can't claim ANY of the VAT from HMRC. You have to ask your contractor to issue a credit note for the overcharged VAT with a new invoice, so make sure that your contractor charges the correct rate of VAT to avoid this situation.

Other VAT recovery issues

If you're a VAT registered business, you may need to adjust how much VAT claimed from HMRC under the "change of use" rules explained in Chapter 19.

Using your own home for holiday lets

If your income from the holiday lets and any other taxable income is less than the VAT registration limit, then you don't have to register for VAT. But of course that means you can't claim VAT on any expenditure.

However you may register on a voluntary basis, in which case you would have to pay VAT on the income from holiday leasing and any other taxable supplies, but you can also claim VAT on related expenditure.

If you are using your own home for holiday lets and you're registered for VAT, there are a few other issues to consider:

- You can only claim VAT on expenditure to the extent that the property is used for business purposes and making taxable supplies. If, for example, you rent out the property for four months each year as holiday lets, then you'd only recover $4/12^{th}$ (i.e. $1/3^{rd}$) of the VAT paid on the property expenditure. See VAT Notice 700, paragraph 4.6 http://tinyurl.com/ot5glbq for further information about VAT on non-business expenditure. If you also receive exempt income from residential lets, then you'd have to apply the complex rules set out in VAT Notice 706: Partial exemption, which includes calculations for business/non-business use as well as the normal partial exemption provisions http://tinyurl.com/mvetpps.

- If you are a director of the company owning the property, then you can only recover VAT on domestic accommodation if it is used for specific business purposes, as explained in VAT Notice 700, paragraph 12.2 http://tinyurl.com/peclox4.
- You may also have to pay additional VAT if you use business assets for personal or other non-business use. See VAT Notice 700, paragraph 9 http://tinyurl.com/qbaoq5x.

In practice, dealing with these issues can be very complicated so please do your research and/or take professional advice before you claim any VAT from HMRC.

Chapter 9: Checklist

- Income from holiday lets is always standard rated, whether or not the property is purpose built or is a dwelling.
- The normal distinction is that planning restrictions or other rules mean that holiday accommodation can't be used as permanent living accommodation.
- Whether a property is a "dwelling" for VAT purposes affects how much VAT you have to pay on the purchase or conversion expenditure
- If it's your own home, then you won't be able to claim all of the VAT on expenditure because the property is used for non-business purposes some of the time.
- VAT exempt income from residential lets can affect the amount of VAT you can recover under the partial exemption rules.
- Purpose built holiday homes are subject to the VAT rules for commercial property rules as explained in Chapter 7.

The 3 step process: Part 2

VAT on expenditure

Chapter 10

How to buy commercial properties VAT free: the VAT 1614D procedure

Buying commercial property to convert to residential use

If you're converting or refurbishing a property, the property itself is usually the single most expensive item. In this chapter, we'll be looking at when and how you can purchase EMPTY commercial properties VAT exempt if you intend to **use them** (i.e. live in as purchased) **or convert** them into dwellings. You can purchase such properties for conversion VAT exempt by issuing a VAT 1614D certificate, as explained in this chapter.

This is a long chapter, but please take the time to read it if you're planning to buy commercial property where the owner has opted to tax. The appendix to this chapter contains answers to the most common FAQs so you should find what you need to know about the VAT1614D procedure here.

YOU NEED TO UNDERSTAND THIS SUBJECT BEFORE YOU EVEN CONSIDER MAKING AN OFFER TO BUY ANY SUCH PROPERTY. OTHERWISE IT MAY BE TOO LATE AND THE VENDOR MAY HAVE TO CHARGE VAT.

- Why do commercial property owners have to charge VAT?
- How to buy opted commercial property VAT exempt: the VAT1614D procedure
- When can I use the VAT1614D?
- How do I do it?
  - When is the price "legally fixed"?
  - When can I issue the VAT 1614D to the vendor?
- Where do I get the form?
- Building land
- Buying as an intermediary
- The vendor's VAT position: the 2-price scenario
- Issuing certificates before the price is legally fixed
- Keep a record of the events and evidence of intent
- What your solicitor needs to know
- Buying VAT free can reduce your stamp duty as well

HMRC guidance: VAT Notice 742a: Opting to tax land and buildings; paragraph 3.4:
http://tinyurl.com/pyn9kuo.

Why do commercial property owners have to charge VAT?

Usually the sale or rent of commercial property is VAT exempt. But there are 2 situations when a commercial property owner has to charge VAT:

- if they are selling the freehold of "new" commercial property; i.e. up to 3 years old; or
- if they have "opted to tax" the property.

"Opting to tax" is a procedure that only applies to commercial property. It means that the owner has to charge VAT if he sells or rents the property and can claim VAT on his costs.

VAT Notice 742a, paragraph 3.7 http://tinyurl.com/p95masr

If you buy a "new" commercial property to convert, then the VAT1614D procedure doesn't apply and you have to pay VAT on the purchase price.

How to buy opted properties VAT exempt

However, if you're planning to live in or convert the property into a dwelling, you can ask the seller not to charge VAT by issuing a VAT1614D certificate. This means that the sale will be exempt from VAT and save 20% on the purchase price. This is often the single largest saving you can make so make sure that you do things right from the start and buy the property exempt.

When can I use the form?

"Designed as a dwelling" is defined in Appendix 2, Definition 1.

You're allowed to use this procedure if you're planning to use as or convert the property into a "dwelling". In this case, the definition of "dwelling" is as follows:

- *the dwelling consists of self-contained living accommodation*
- *there is no provision for direct internal access from the dwelling to any other dwelling or part of a dwelling*
- *the separate use of the dwelling is not prohibited by the terms of any covenant, statutory planning consent or similar provision, and*
- *the separate disposal of the dwelling is not prohibited by the terms of any covenant, statutory planning consent or similar provision*

What if I'm buying land to build property?

You can't use the VAT 1614 procedure to buy building land, unless it's for personal or family use. If you pay VAT, you can claim it if you use the land to make zero-rated (or other taxable) sales, such as the sale of new dwellings.

How do I use the VAT 1614D?

In principle, it's a very simple process. If you issue the certificate VAT1614D to the vendor **BEFORE THE PRICE IS LEGALLY FIXED** the vendor <u>must</u> sell the property VAT exempt. If you issue the certificate after this date, but before completion, the vendor MAY accept it, but it's not compulsory. See the FAQs for more information.

What is "legally fixed"?

When you buy a property, the price is usually "legally fixed" when contracts are exchanged. I'll refer to "exchange of contracts" in this chapter, but prices can be "legally fixed" in other ways, such as payment of a non-refundable deposit.

Ask your solicitor to confirm if you're in any doubt about this.

Issuing the VAT 1614D certificate doesn't mean that you're legally bound to buy the property. It simply means that the vendor MUST sell the property VAT exempt to you if you issue the certificate before the price is "legally fixed".

When can I issue the VAT 1614D certificate?

I always advise purchasers <u>to issue their certificates as soon as they are considering making an offer for the property to make sure that the vendor is aware of their intention</u>. It's better to issue a certificate early in the process even if you don't end up buying the property.

This often means that you'll be issuing the certificate to the vendor before you've made an offer to buy the property, but it doesn't bind you to buying the property.

See the appendix to this chapter if you're buying at auction.

You should also read HMRC's guidance about this issue: VAT Notice 742a; Opting to tax land and buildings, paragraph 3.4:

http://tinyurl.com/ohdxqsz

N.B. You can also use the VAT1614D procedure if you're buying as a **"relative intermediary"** for a third party, e.g. if the purchaser wants to remain anonymous. See VAT Notice 742a, paragraph s3.4.5 http://tinyurl.com/ohdxqsz

Where do I get the form?

You can download form VAT1614D from the HMRC website http://tinyurl.com/p7xl5n7.

The form is a two-sided A4 document, which requires the name and address of both vendor and purchaser, as well as details of the property itself.

The vendor's VAT position: the 2 price scenario

The vendor may want to increase the sales price if the sale is exempt, because selling exempt means that the vendor may have to pay VAT previously claimed on costs back to HMRC

This can include VAT costs incurred up to 10 years in the past. Sometimes the amounts involved may be relatively small and the vendor will be willing to bear the cost. However in other cases it could be a significant amount, perhaps several thousands, tens of thousands of pounds or even more.

Also, selling VAT exempt means that the vendor may not be able to claim VAT on costs relating to the sale, e.g. legal fees or auctioneer's fees.

Sometimes vendors increase the price if you issue a VAT1614D because they have to repay some VAT to HMRC if they sell the property VAT exempt.

That's why vendors sometimes quote 2 different sales prices: an "exempt" sales price which is usually higher to take account of any VAT he may have to repay to HMRC; and a "taxable" sales price which is lower.

There's nothing in the VAT legislation that prevents this. Ultimately the price is a matter of negotiation between you and the vendor like any other aspect of the property purchase.

See "And if you have to pay VAT..." at the end of the Chapter 10 Appendix to this chapter where I've discussed this situation in more detail.

Keep a record of the events and evidence of intent

Remember to keep a copy of any VAT1614D certificates you issue. You should also retain correspondence and other documentation that demonstrate your intention to use or convert the property into a dwelling or other residential property, in case HMRC asks the vendor for such information at a later date.

This information could include applications for planning permission or other correspondence with the local planning office, or quotes from contractors for the conversion work. HMRC DO check up on such documentation and *will require a vendor to charge VAT AFTER THE EVENT if they aren't satisfied that the evidence doesn't reflect that the property would be used for residential use after purchase.*

What does my solicitor need to know?

You should tell your solicitor that you want to purchase the property VAT exempt as soon as possible, particularly if the vendor wants to charge a higher selling price if his option to tax is disapplied.

Your solicitor will be involved throughout the process, so you need to be sure that they understand how the procedure works and why it's essential that the certificate is issued before the price has been legally fixed.

Buying VAT free can reduce your stamp duty as well

Stamp duty land tax is paid on the VAT inclusive value of the purchase. So by purchasing the property VAT exempt, your SDLT cost is also reduced.

Your solicitor will be dealing with the SDLT side of things so ensure that he/she is aware that you intend to purchase the property VAT exempt from the start so they can ensure that you pay the correct amount of SDLT.

> It's an offence to isssue a VAT 1614D certificate incorrectly and HMRC can issue penalties if you make invalid declarations on the form.

See VAT Notice 742: Land and property, paragraph 7.10
http://tinyurl.com/bswtrlp

What if I have to pay VAT on the property?

If you don't issue the VAT 1614D on time, or you're buying a "new" commercial property (i.e. up to 3 years since completion), you'll have to pay VAT at 20%.

So if you have to pay VAT on the property, then make sure that you aren't charged too much VAT.

- When you have to pay VAT: The "90/10" split

What if the property includes existing residential areas, e.g. dwellings? In this case, the normal rule is that vendors should only charge VAT on the commercial parts of mixed properties, because the sale of the residential part is exempt from VAT. You should agree this apportionment as early as possible through the negotiation process. It will also help minimise any stamp duty land tax liability because this is paid on the VAT inclusive purchase price.

In the case of public houses, industry practice is to treat 90% of the property price as business and 10% as domestic for VAT purposes. This means that you'd normally be charged VAT on 90% of the property cost.

However, as far as I'm aware, there's no legal basis for this and HMRC state in their internal guidance that this apportionment should not apply if it's clearly inappropriate. So ask the vendor to apportion the selling price on a more accurate basis, for example based on the relative proportions of floor area.

Chapter 10: Appendix

VAT 1614D: FAQs

It's difficult to anticipate every possible scenario, but these are some of the most commonly asked questions about using the VAT1614D certificate

- What if I'm buying at auction?
- Do I need planning permission for conversion work before I issue the VAT1614D?
- What happens if I'm late with my certificate?
- What if I don't use the property as intended when I bought it?
- What if the property contains an existing dwelling(s)?
- What if there are tenants in the property?
- Buying VAT exempt in other situations
- What if I'm buying a "new" commercial property to convert into a home?

What if I'm buying at auction?

One of the most common issues is how the certification procedure works when you're buying a property at auction.

There are no special rules for property purchases at auctions. I'd suggest that you contact the auction house in advance to ask if they have any special procedures for VAT 1614D certificates if you're planning to bid.

The same VAT1614D rules apply if you're buying at auction.

You can issue a VAT1614D in advance if you're planning to make a bid.

If you're in any doubt, you can always issue the certificate to the vendor BEFORE the date of the auction, even if you don't know whether the vendor has opted to tax.

Alternatively, the vendor may, as explained below, accept a "late" certificate as long as it is received before the sale is completed.

Do I need planning permission for the conversion before issuing the certificate?

No. *It's the <u>intention at the time of purchase</u> to use or convert the property as or convert to a dwelling that entitles a purchaser to ask the vendor to sell the property VAT free*

What happens if I'm late with my certificate?

The vendor *may* also agree to accept a certificate which is received after the date on which the price is "legally fixed", as long as it is <u>before completion</u> of the sale. Notice 742a, paragraph 3.4.4 explains this in further detail <u>http://tinyurl.com/p7xl5n7</u>.

However, you can't force the vendor to accept a certificate once the price is legally fixed. Vendors may not want to accept late certificates if it means that they have to repay VAT on their costs to HMRC.

What if I don't use the property as intended when I bought it?

I'm often asked by purchasers if they have to pay VAT if their plans fall through; e.g if they don't get planning permission for their conversion.

The good news is that you DON'T have to pay the VAT

This is one of the main issues that concerns purchasers. Potential purchasers often assume that if they don't get planning permission or can't raise the funding for the conversion, or have to rent the property out before doing any work, they will have to pay the VAT they saved on the purchase.

No. And there is a logical reason for this.

Purchasers issue VAT 1614 certificates because their <u>intention at the point of purchase</u> is to use the property for residential purposes. Even if things don't go to plan and the property is not used as intended, the VAT exempt liability is fixed at the point of sale.

> The VAT 1614D certificate is a legal document. Only issue if you genuinely INTEND to live in or convert the property into a dwelling or for "relevant residential" purposes.

Surely HMRC will lose out on tax revenue if I purchase a property for conversion but ultimately use it for commercial purposes?

That is how the law works. It isn't your VAT cost.

BUT remember that the certificate is a legal document, so only issue it if you genuinely intend to live in or convert the property into a dwelling. If HMRC suspect that the certificate has been used erroneously, they will ask the vendor to provide evidence to confirm whether or not there was a genuine intention to use as or convert the property into a dwelling at the time of purchase.

What if there's already a dwelling at the property?

The sale of self-contained existing dwellings, whether a house or a flat, is always VAT exempt. So if the property contains a commercial property and a dwelling - e.g. a flat above a shop, the vendor should apportion the price and exempt the proportion that relates to the flat. The option to tax only applies to the commercial part; in other words the vendor can only charge VAT on the proportion of the sales price that relates to the shop, or pub, or office etc. But you can issue the certificate if you intend to use the whole or part of the property as a dwelling or convert it to create an additional dwelling.

What if there are tenants in the property?

Buying tenanted property - whether wholly or partly tenanted - is normally regarded as the purchase of a business as a going concern ("TOGC")vfor VAT purposes, not the purchase of a property. The rules for TOGCs are quite different and potentially complicated. You may still be able to purchase the property VAT free as the purchase of a business as a going concern, but it would be under a different set of rules and the VAT 1614D procedure will not apply. In that situation, I'd strongly recommend that you take professional advice.

What if I'm buying a "new" commercial building?

If you're purchasing a new commercial property to convert to a dwelling, you will have to pay the VAT.

And if you have to pay VAT....

I've recently dealt with a situation where a company issued a VAT 1614D certificate to a vendor to buy a £1m property to convert to residential VAT exempt. The vendor explained that if the sale was VAT exempt, then the sales price would increase to £1.1m because the vendor would have to repay £100,000 VAT to HMRC. The vendor has recently purchased an extended 150 year lease in the property and claimed VAT on the lease premium.

So in this case, the purchasers' options are either to pay £1.1m VAT exempt, or to pay £1m plus 20% VAT £200,000, buying the property as a taxable purchase. This might seem to make the deal unworkable, but as I've explained below, there are ways in which you can claim the VAT from HMRC.

The buyer's decision will almost certainly depend on whether or not they can claim the 20% VAT from HMRC. This may be possible if the buyer converts the properties to dwellings and sells a long lease in the dwellings. In this case, the sale of the newly converted dwellings may qualify for the zero-rate if they fall within the criteria for the sale or non-residential conversions explained in <u>Chapter 8</u>. Alternatively, if the developer wants to use the dwellings as investment properties, then they may consider setting up a separate leasing company and selling the long leases to the leasing company which will own the short term leases with the tenants.

Setting up leasing companies and other "planning" arrangements is not prohibited under VAT legislation, although there are certain anti-avoidance provisions that can sometimes apply to transactions between associated businesses. However the issues can be complex and also have to consider other tax and accounting factors. Also, you have to be able to fund the VAT on the initial purchase until you're able to claim the VAT from HMRC.

The point is that ***paying VAT on a property purchase isn't necessarily a deal breaker***. Like any other cost, the VAT on a property purchase can be claimed VAT if the property is used to generate taxable supplies. You have options.

If you're in this situation, I'd strongly recommend that you take professional advice to ensure that the arrangements are set up correctly and that the transactions have the necessary VAT liability.

Chapter 10: Checklist

- The option to tax doesn't apply to existing dwellings or other residential properties. The vendor can't charge VAT on the proportion of the sales price relating to those parts of the building even if he's opted to tax the property.
- If you want to convert a commercial property into a dwellings, you MUST issue a VAT 1614D certificate to the seller to buy the property VAT exempt.
- The certificate MUST be issued before the price is legally fixed to ensure that the option to tax is disapplied. The seller <u>may</u> agree to accept a certificate issued at any time up until completion.
- You don't have to have planning permission to convert the property to issue the VAT 1614D. Your <u>intention</u> at the time of the purchase determines the right to issue the certificate.
- The certificate is a legal document and there are legal penalties for using it incorrectly. If you're the purchaser, you should retain other documentary evidence, e.g. correspondence with architects, enquiries about planning permission to support the use of the certificate.
- Buying a property VAT exempt can also reduce your stamp duty.
- There are special rules for the purchase of tenanted properties.
- You don't have to pay the VAT to HMRC if you don't use the property as you'd intended when you bought it.
- If you still have to pay VAT on a property purchase, it's not necessarily a deal breaker as you may be able to claim it from HMRC.

Chapter 11

Zero rating new construction services

The chapter explains when construction services qualify for the zero-rate.

- How does it work in practice?
  - Consider VAT at the planning stage
- Definitions: "qualifying properties
- When does the zero-rate apply?
  - Are you creating a NEW dwelling?
  - Zero-rated construction services

How does it work in practice?

In this chapter, we'll be focusing on the construction of single household dwellings. Most of the principles also apply to property used for "relevant residential purposes" and certain properties used for "relevant charitable purposes".

Normally, construction work on existing property work is liable to VAT at 20%, so if the net cost of the construction is £10,000, the VAT would be £2,000; if it's £100,000 then the VAT would be £20,000 and so on and so on. So if your construction work qualifies for the zero-rate, the VAT can contribute a significant amount to your profits, as shown in the case study.

Consider the VAT liability at the planning stage

It's important to consider the VAT liability at the planning stage because it will affect the initial funding requirements, as well as ongoing budgeting throughout the project. As we've seen throughout this book, even small differences in layout, use, planning permission, function can all make a significant difference to the overall VAT cost.

Once the plans are approved by the planning office and the construction work is underway, it's usually too late to make changes and developers are stuck with a VAT bill – for an additional 5% or even 20% - that could have been avoided if the VAT liability was considered earlier.

- Involve your architects in the process as early as possible and ensure that they understand how the VAT rules apply. Sometimes minor changes to the design can bring a development into the zero-rate or the reduced rate and they may able to identify other adjustments that might help reduce the VAT cost.

- If you're applying for planning permission, discuss issues that could affect VAT with the planning office.
- If you and/or your architects have even the slightest doubt, take advice. Investing in good advice at this stage can help to save a lot of money in the longer term. The cost will almost certainly be covered by the VAT savings or at least by helping to avoid expensive mistakes.

If you have to pay VAT, it's better to know in advance in case the VAT cost has a major effect on the project's overall financial viability.

Definitions

"Qualifying properties"

The zero-rate and reduced rate reliefs for construction services apply to "qualifying properties", which are defined in the legislation as dwellings, properties used for "relevant residential purposes" (including bedsits and other "multi-occupancy dwellings") and "relevant charitable purposes". The legal definitions of all of these are included in Appendix 2.

It's important that both developers and contractors consider whether the properties fall within these definitions at the planning stage to avoid unexpected VAT expenditure at a later date.

When does the zero-rate apply?

The construction of new dwellings usually qualifies for the zero-rate, but only if all of the criteria are met. The rules themselves are explained in detail in VAT Notice 708, section 3 http://tinyurl.com/mdc8465. The basic conditions are as follows:

- A qualifying building has been, is being, or will be constructed - i.e. a dwelling, property used for "relevant residential purposes" or "relevant charitable purposes" property as explained above;
- the services are made "in the course of the construction" of that building - this normally means that the work is done before completion of the construction;
- where necessary, the developer issues a valid certificate to the contractor; - certificates must be issued if the contractor's services are constructing property used for "relevant residential purposes" or "relevant charitable purposes", not dwellings; and
- there services are not specifically excluded from zero-rating; for example legal and architects' services are specifically excluded from the zero-rate.

VAT Notice 708, section 3 includes a lot more detailed information, so please make sure that you've read section 3 properly for the important details.

Are you creating a NEW dwelling?

The next thing is to consider if you're actually creating a <u>new</u> dwelling. So what if you're replacing an existing dwelling on the same site? In this case, the normal rule is that the original property must have been demolished to at least ground level.

If you're planning a conversion which will create ADDITIONAL dwellings, the first thing to consider is whether or not the zero-rate could apply to the construction work.

The zero-rate applies when new residential properties are created by extending or enlarging an existing property, but **ONLY if the new property is entirely contained within the new extension**.

In other words, if any part of the new dwelling is within the footprint of the existing property, even just a small area, none of the construction qualifies for the zero-rate.

HMRC's guidance on this subject is very comprehensive; especially Notice 708, sections 3.2.1 to 3.2.4 http://tinyurl.com/k6asmpr.

Section 3.2.4 says:

*"You can zero-rate the enlargement of, or extension to, an existing building **to the extent** that the extension or enlargement contains an additional dwelling **provided**:*

- *the new dwelling is wholly within the enlargement or extension; and*
- *the dwelling is 'designed as a dwelling' – see paragraph 14.2.*

So, for example, a new eligible flat built on top of an existing building can be zero-rated."

This means that if you construct a new dwelling which includes any part of an existing dwelling, whether it's part of the hallway, the garage, a vertical slice dividing the existing dwelling, then the construction of the new dwelling does NOT qualify for zero-rating.

The inclusion of any other part of the existing property, however small, prevents the construction qualifying as "new". The only exception is the inclusion of party walls and, in certain cases, facades which must be retained as a condition of the planning permission.

N.B. If the zero-rate doesn't apply, then check out whether the creation of additional dwellings incorporating parts of an existing property qualify for the reduced rate as a qualifying conversion as explained in Chapter 12.

Zero-rated construction services

Zero-rating for new construction covers a wide range of services:

- Work on the building itself, including normal decoration work done prior to completion.
- Work that is closely connected to the construction of the building.

Zero-rating applies to a wide range of services from demolishing an existing property as part of a single contract to construct new properties on the site; to the construction of new roads, pavements for access to the new property and basic landscaping, up to and including laying turf.

Services provided by subcontractors can qualify for the zero-rate as well as main contractors. However this only applies for services carried out to dwellings, not PROPERTY USED FOR "relevant residential purposes" or "relevant charitable purposes".

See VAT Notice 708 section 3.3 http://tinyurl.com/kgh9wgs for HMRC's guidance about services made "in the course of construction" and when they qualify for the zero-rate

The zero-rate DOES NOT apply to professional services in connection with new construction, so you have to factor VAT at 20% into your budget for architects, legal and accountancy services. But you might consider a "design and build" arrangement where a main contractor employs all of the professionals and supplies a single supply of zero-rated construction services - see VAT Notice 708, section 3.4.1. http://tinyurl.com/mdc8465.

There's more information about zero-rating in Chapters 11 - 14 and the FAQs in Chapter 21, so make sure that you read those chapters as well. The zero-rate usually applies to goods and materials incorporated into the new property by the contractor, if they qualify as "building materials". See Chapters 15 and 21 which explain the goods that qualify as "building materials".

Chapter 11: Checklist

- The construction of certain new residential properties is zero-rated.
- These include dwellings and properties used for "relevant residential purposes" or "relevant charitable purposes".
- The zero-rate only applies if the construction creates an entirely NEW property.
- The zero-rate applies to a wide range of services in the course of construction.
- The zero-rate also applies to "building materials" supplied and installed by the contractor in the course of the zero-rated construction work.

Chapter 12

Reduced rated conversions and renovations

In this chapter, we'll be looking at the situations when the reduced rate can apply for conversions and renovations and the services that qualify.

- Reduced rate for qualifying conversions.
- Reduced rate for qualifying renovations.
- Which conversion and renovation services qualify for the reduced rate?
  - Qualifying services.

When does the 5% rate apply?

The 5% rate applies to conversions to change the number of dwellings or property used for "relevant residential purposes" in existing buildings OR to renovations of existing dwellings or property used for "relevant residential" purposes that haven't been occupied in for the past 2 years. These include both single household dwellings and multi-occupancy dwellings, such as bedsits.

The reduced rate of 5% represents a substantial saving on the standard rate.

What types of property conversions or renovations qualify for relief?

Qualifying conversions

The reduced rate applies when all 3 of the following conditions, as defined in the legislation, are met:

- It must be a "qualifying conversion".
- The contractor's services are "qualifying services".
- In the case of work relating to RRP properties, the developer must issue a certificate confirming that the work is eligible for the reduced rate.

The main principles are that the conversion must:

- change the number of single household dwellings in any property; or

- create a new multi-occupancy dwelling (i.e. a property containing multi-occupancy dwellings, not additional units); or
- a "special residential conversion" which normally means creating a new property used for "relevant residential purposes". This doesn't include adding a building to existing residential home.

For example:

- creating dwellings or property used for "relevant residential purposes" from commercial properties;
- changing the number of single household dwellings; e.g. converting a house into a number of flats or extending a house to create an additional house; and
- converting a property into a multiple occupancy dwelling; e.g. converting an office into a bedsit block.

HMRC's examples include the conversion of:

- *a property that has never been lived in, such as an office block or a barn;*
- *a multiple occupancy building such as a bedsit block;*
- *living accommodation which is not self-contained, such as a pub containing staff accommodation that is not self-contained; and*
- *any dwelling which had previously been adapted in its entirety to another use, such as to offices or a dental practice.*

There's a useful decision table in VAT Notice 708, sections 7.2 and 7.3 http://tinyurl.com/pyyo2e7 to help you decide whether the reduced rate applies to your development.

When conversions aren't conversions

As I explained in Chapter 2, the word "conversion" has two distinct meanings in the context of construction and property.

- The first is the application of the reduced rate to conversion services as listed above.
- The second is the conversion of commercial properties into certain residential properties; i.e. "non-residential conversions". The freehold sale or grant of a long lease of certain non-residential conversions can qualify for zero-rating, which enables the developer to claim VAT on related costs. See Chapter 8 for further information about "non-residential conversions".

The "conversion" criteria are completely separate and your conversion may apply for just one of the reliefs. For example, suppose you've converted a mixed property to create new dwellings incorporating parts of the existing residential areas. In this case, the conversion wouldn't qualify as a "non-residential conversion" so the sales of the converted dwellings wouldn't qualify for zero-rating. This means you wouldn't be able to claim VAT paid on the conversion costs. However some or all of the conversion work would probably qualify for the reduced rate of 5% if you're creating additional dwellings in the property.

Also, see the Appendix to Chapter 8 I've given some examples of when the different definitions apply.

See Chapter 13 for more details about when the reduced rate applies, e.g. if you're converting and refurbishing a property at the same time.

What sort of renovations qualify for the reduced rate?

Qualifying renovations and alterations

The reduced rate applies to the supply, in the course of the renovation or alteration of qualifying residential premises, of qualifying services related to the renovation or alteration.

All of the following conditions must be met:

o   The work is done on "qualifying residential premises".
o   The premises haven't been occupied (i.e. lived in) for two years or longer; the "two year rule".
o   The contractor's services are "qualifying services".
o   In the case of work relating to RRP properties, the developer must issue a certificate to the contractor confirming that the work is eligible for the reduced rate.

.

"Qualifying residential premises" includes those listed in section 8.2 of Notice 708 http://tinyurl.com/pyyo2e7, including single household dwellings, multi-occupancy dwellings and property used for "relevant residential purposes".

Empty home conditions

The properties must also satisfy one of the "Empty Home Conditions" . The main conditions of these are:

The first "empty home condition" applies to empty premises, where the property has been continuously "empty" in the two years immediately before the contractor starts work. So if you're a contractor and you start renovation work on 1 April 2017, you can charge the reduced rate as long as the property was empty for at least 2 years from 1 April 2015 to 31 March 2017.

HMRC has also confirmed that the reduced rate can apply to work carried out AFTER the property is occupied AS LONG AS the work starts at least one day before the property is occupied. See VAT Notice 708, para 8.3.4 http://tinyurl.com/mod94mc.

Example Suppose that the property was empty from 1 April 2015 to 31 March 2107. The property was purchased by the new owner on 1 April 2017 and they move in on 10 April. In this case, the contractor can charge the reduced rate as long as the work starts on 9 April or earlier.

The second "empty home condition" applies to the renovation of occupied "single household dwellings". It applies if the property was empty for two years before it was purchased and the work commences after the date it was re-occupied *by the person who purchased the property.*

In this case, the reduced rate can apply if the following 4 conditions are met:

- In the two years immediately before the occupier acquired the dwelling it had not been lived in.
- No renovation or alteration had been carried out in the two years before the occupier acquired the dwelling (ignoring any minor works that were necessary to keep the dwelling dry and secure).
- The contractor's services are supplied to the occupier, which means that sub-contractors must always charge the standard rate; i.e. 20% VAT on their work.
- The work is completed within 1 year of the occupier acquiring the welling.

In other words, if the new owner moved in before you start your work, the reduced rate can apply if the work as long as finished within 1 year of the occupier acquiring the dwelling and the other conditions are met.

Example If the new owner purchased and occupied the property on 1 April 2017 and you started work on 10 April, you can charge the reduced rate as long as the work is finished by 31 March 2018.

Remember that in this situation, the reduced rate applies only when the services are provided to the new owner and only applies to single household dwellings, not property used for "relevant residential purposes" or other multi-occupancy properties.

See VAT Notice 708, section 8.3 for further information about the "empty home conditions" http://tinyurl.com/o96acdw, including details of certain types of occupation that can be "ignored".

Which services qualify for the reduced rate?

The reduced rate applies to a broad range of work, from redecoration, repairs, extensions, alterations, as shown in the box on the next page.

However <u>the scope of the reduced rate for conversions and renovations is less generous than the zero-rate for new construction</u>. For example, the zero-rate applies to certain landscaping/gardening work done in the course of new construction, but the reduced rate does NOT apply for such work in conversions and renovations.

> **Qualifying services**
>
> The reduced rate applies to the "qualifying services" carried out in the course of "qualifying conversions" or "qualifying renovations".
>
> Qualifying services:
>
> The services that qualify for the reduced rate fall within two categories:
>
> 1. works to the fabric of the building; such as redecoration, repair, maintenance or improvement; and
> 2. works within the immediate site in connection with the provision of :
>   - water, heat, power or access;
>   - drainage or security; or
>   - waste disposal
>
>   to the building.

Work to the fabric of the building. HMRC give some very helpful examples of the services that are covered by the reduced rate done in the course of the qualifying conversion or renovation/alteration, which include:

- Alterations, such as extensions to the property or the installation of double glazing
- Redecoration and maintenance of the property.

Work within the "Immediate site" generally means the immediate area around a property that is "used for the comfortable enjoyment" of the property", according to HMRC's staff manuals. There's no other definition for this term, so it's a matter of interpretation. For example, the installation of pipes or cables underneath the surrounding garden to connect the property to the mains supplies would probably qualify, but extending the pipes or cables any further – for example under pavements or roads to connect to the mains services wouldn't be regarded as being within the "immediate site".

In practice the VAT liability of this sort of expenditure – where it's a matter of interpretation - is often referred to the Tax Tribunal when HMRC and the contractor can't agree.

Also, the reduced rate only applies to goods and materials that are "building materials" when supplied and installed by contractors in the course of the qualifying construction, conversion or renovation.

See Chapter 15 and Chapter 21 (FAQs) for information about building materials and other related services.

 See Notice 708, sections 7.6 http://tinyurl.com/ngqwlb9 and 8.4 http://tinyurl.com/p77l9zj for HMRC's guidance about the services that qualify for the reduced rate.

Chapter 12

- The reduced rate applies to the following conversions:
  - Change number of single household dwellings in a property
  - Creating new multi-occupancy dwellings
  - Change to a new relevant residential property
- The reduced rate also applies to the renovation or alteration of existing dwellings that have been unoccupied for at least two years.
- The reduced rate applies to certain "qualifying services" including work to the fabric of the property and certain services relating to the provision of heat, power, water and other utilities.
- The definition of "conversion" subject to the reduced rate is NOT THE SAME as the definition of "conversion" of properties which are zero-rated when sold – see the Appendix to Chapter 2.

Chapter 13

Mixed residential developments, standard rated conversion services and other practical issues

In this part, we'll be looking at some more complicated aspects of the VAT liability of conversions and renovations.

- Which rate of VAT applies to conversions and renovations of the same property?
  - o The Note 3(3) issue
  - o Converting horizontally
  - o Converting vertically
- What's <u>always</u> standard rated even in zero-rated new construction and reduced rated qualifying conversions and renovations?
- When is "completion"?
- Mixed developments: apportioning the price between work at different rates.
  - o Work done before completion
  - o Work done after completion
- Garages.
- Planning permission; building consents: why it matters.

Which rate of VAT applies to conversions and renovations of the same property "

Developers often assume that the reduced rate applies to all of the work done to a property if the work changes the number of dwellings in that property. Unfortunately, it's not that simple.

The Note 3(3) issue

There is a specific rule that says that the reduced rate only applies to conversions if the work changes the number of dwellings in that particular <u>part</u> of the building. The legal reference is VAT Act 1994, Schedule 7A, Group 6, Note 3(3). I'll refer to it as the "Note 3(3) issue".

What exactly does it mean? Suppose you convert a house into 2 separate flats. You'd assume that the whole conversion would be liable to the reduced rate. However, that's not how it works. Under Note 3(3), you have to look at each part of the property separately. And that's why the VAT rate of certain conversions is 5% and others 20%, even if they seem to create the same number of new dwellings.

<u>Example One</u>

Suppose you buy an old public house which contains an apartment on the first floor which was recently occupied by the pub's landlord.   Your initial plan is to convert the ground floor into a separate apartment.

Converting horizontally

In this case, the ground floor and the first floor could be regarded as separate parts, so the VAT liability of the conversion services is as follows:

- The conversion of the ground floor will qualify for the reduced rate because the number of dwellings changes from zero to one.
- If you convert the entire property into a single dwelling, the work wouldn't qualify for relief at all because the building as a whole has the same number of dwellings after the conversion as before.

But what if the living accommodation isn't self-contained, such as a pub containing staff accommodation?   In this case, if you convert the property into one or more separate dwellings, the construction services should qualify for the reduced rate of VAT.

Converting vertically

Going back to our original example of the pub with a first floor apartment. What would be the liability of construction services if you split the property down the middle to create 2 houses?

In this case, because of Note 3(3), I think that HMRC's view would be that the work to the first floor would qualify for the reduced rate and the work to the ground floor would be liable to the standard rate. The legislation means that is that it's not only necessary for the number of single household dwellings in the property as a whole to change; but the conversion has to result in a changed number of single household dwellings in each "part" of the property.

In our case, each floor would be a "part" because it's got a floor, walls and ceiling and is large enough to contain a single household dwelling. Therefore the VAT liability of conversion services would be as follows:

- Ground floor: This contains no single household dwellings before the conversion and no single household dwellings after the conversion. Therefore my interpretation is that the reduced rate doesn't apply so the contractor would have to charge VAT at 20% on work done to this floor.

- First floor: Before the conversion this contained one single household dwelling, but after the conversion doesn't contain a single household dwelling. Instead, it contains two halves of separate single household dwellings. Therefore the number of SINGLE HOUSEHOLD dwellings in this part of the property has changed from one to zero and the reduced rate applies to the conversion work on the first floor.

This means that in this example, it appears that the proportion of the work that qualifies for the reduced rate is the same <u>whether the conversion is done horizontally or vertically</u>. But every situation is different and you may interpret the rules in a different way, so you need to consider your development in its own right.

<u>Example Two</u>

A property contains two maisonettes, on the ground floor and the first one. You decide to convert the first floor into two apartments while completely refurbishing the ground floor, adding an extension and changing the lay out.

In this case, I think that some or all of the work done on the first floor can be at 5% because the number of dwellings has increased from one to two. The work done to refurbish and remodel the ground floor doesn't qualify for the reduced rate as a conversion because there's no change to the number of dwellings in that part of the building.

HMRC give more examples about this issue in Notice 708, s7.3.1 http://tinyurl.com/q5paww8 which includes a detailed case study that is very helpful. If you're in any doubt about your own development, I'd recommend investing in professional advice and/or asking HMRC for a ruling as soon as possible in the process.

What's always standard rated: Goods that aren't "building materials"

The zero-rating of new residential properties and reduced rating for qualifying conversions and renovations extends to the supply and installation certain goods that are incorporated into the new property in the course of the construction or conversion or renovation. These goods are referred to as "builder's materials" in the VAT legislation.

These is explained in some detail in VAT Notice 708, section 13 http://tinyurl.com/mohugtx.

The supply of, or supply and installation of goods that aren't building materials is always standard rated. Some of the best known examples are fitted furniture (other than kitchen units) and carpets. The effect of the rule is to prevent the reduced rate or zero-rate from applying to anything other than "building materials". I've explained more about the meaning of "building materials" in Chapter 15, but this is how the law applies to such goods and materials:

If you're a contractor and you're carrying out new construction which qualifies for the zero-rate, or a qualifying conversion or renovation which qualifies for the reduced rate, the zero-rate or reduced rate applies to "building materials" supplied with those services. However the zero-rate may apply to the service of installing the goods in the course of new construction, even if the goods themselves are standard rated.

If you're a developer and are purchasing goods for incorporation into properties which you're currently converting or refurbishing, you can't claim VAT on these goods. VAT on installation services can be claimed under the normal rules (see Chapters 17 - 20).

See Chapter 15 for more information about building materials. The detailed rules about "building materials" are in VAT Notice 708, sections 11 – 14, including detailed lists of items that are regarded as "building materials" in dwellings at section 13.8.1 http://tinyurl.com/kc24l78.

Completion

The date of completion of any development is important, because work done after completion is liable to VAT at 20%. So when is completion?

HMRC explain that completion depends on the circumstances of the specific development but that the following factors will be taken into account:

- *when a Certificate of Completion is issued;*
- *the accordance to approved plans and specifications;*
- *the scope of the planning consent and variations to it; and*
- *whether the building is habitable or fit for purpose.*

HMRC also give some examples of when they consider work to be done "in the course of construction" in VAT Notice 708, section 3.3.2 http://tinyurl.com/kgh9wgs. It includes "snagging" which is usually carried out after completion.

N.B. HMRC's guidance relates to new construction. However the same principles apply to conversions and renovations.

Apportioning expenditure for mixed rate services

There are two situations when contractors have to apportion their charges:

- when the work includes different rates; such as a reduced rated conversions which includes some standard rated work <u>before completion</u>; and
- when a zero-rated new construction or reduced rated contract continues <u>after completion</u> of the project.

In either case, if the contractor doesn't identify work that qualifies for the zero-rate or reduced rate separately, then he must charge VAT at 20% on the total amount.

Work done before completion

A mixed supply includes work done at different rates of VAT. Contractors can apportion the cost for work on these parts of the property "to the extent that it relates to the qualifying parts" and charge the zero-rate or reduced rate on that value of the work. Otherwise, they must charge 20% on the full value.

- Work on specific parts of the property

If your development includes a reduced rated conversion and a standard rated renovation within a single property, the contractor must specify the value of work that qualifies for the reduced rate, or charge VAT on the total amount.

- Common parts of the property

Work on those parts of the property that are common to all of the individual residential units is regarded by HMRC as a mixed supply. This could include work to the common areas of the building, such as the roof, foundations, the plumbing and heating systems, lifts, the entrance lobby and similar parts. The contractor can apportion his charge for this work and charge the reduced rate on the proportion that relates to the reduced rated conversion.

How should the contractor apportion his price for work on those parts?

Contractors can apportion expenditure for such work between different liabilities using any method as long as it gives a "fair and reasonable" result.

Apportionment based on based on floor area is sometimes used, where the price is apportioned by reference to the floor areas of new construction, qualifying conversions and renovations and other work.

HMRC's guidance on this subject in respect of construction work is VAT Notice, Section 16: Apportionment for part qualifying buildings http://tinyurl.com/q6wz4vl covers this subject in some detail.

If you're a contractor, you should read HMRC's guidance about this issue carefully and take advice or as HMRC for a ruling if they have any concerns about how the apportionment rules apply in particular situations.

Work done after completion

Work done after completion is usually liable to VAT at the standard rate, except as explained in VAT Notice 708, s3.2.1 and certain renovation services as explained below.

Garages

If the conversion or renovation works explained in this chapter include work to garages, then the reduced rate also applies in the
following circumstances:

Conversions

- converting an existing outbuilding into a garage;
- building a new detached garage and
- building a drive to serve the garage.

The garage MUST be occupied or intended for occupation with the new or newly converted dwelling AND the work must be done before completion.

See VAT Notice 708, section 7.6.1 http://tinyurl.com/ngqwlb9 for HMRC's guidance on the subject.

Renovations

Similar provisions apply when work is carried out to garages at the same time as qualifying renovations; including
- renovating an existing garage;
- building a new garage; or
- converting an existing building into a garage.

The garage has to be intended for occupation with the newly renovated/altered dwelling. See VAT Notice 708, s8.4.1 http://tinyurl.com/p77l9zj.

Chapter 13: Checklist

- The VAT liability of conversion work depends on each individual case. Contractors have to identify whether their work has changed the number of single household dwellings in a property or part of a property.
- Contractors can apportion the cost of their work between work at different rates of VAT and the zero-rate or the reduced rate on the respective amounts. However if the invoice does not identify separate values of work at different rates, then the contractor must charge 20% VAT on the total value of the invoice.
- The supply and installation of "builders' materials" that are incorporated into the property in the course of construction/conversion or renovation can be zero-rated or reduced rated.
- Goods that are not "builder's materials" are always standard rated.
- The zero-rate and reduced rate for construction services only apply if the conditions for the VAT reliefs are reflected in planning permission, building consents and similar permissions.

Chapter 14

Subcontractors, paying in cash and other money issues

In this part, we'll be discussing other practical issues, including:

- Subcontractors
  - o Can subcontractors charge the reduced rate?
  - o Work on "certified" properties is always standard rated
  - o Does it matter whether subcontractors charge the correct VAT rate if I can claim the VAT from HMRC?
- What happens if the contractor wants to charge me 20% but I think that the 5% rate should apply?
- What if we're still unsure about the VAT liability of certain work?
- Does it matter if I can claim the VAT on my VAT return?
- Surely it's cheaper using unregistered suppliers?
  - o It depends on the mix of goods and services
- Paying in cash.
- Pub conversions.

Subcontractors

> One of the most common queries I get from contractors or developers is how to deal with the VAT liability of services provided by subcontractors. There are 2 main issues:
>
> - Should subcontractors working on qualifying conversions or renovations charge the reduced rate of VAT; and
> - Can contractors claim VAT overcharged by subcontractors on such jobs?

To answer the second question first, <u>you can NEVER claim VAT which has been incorrectly charged.</u> It doesn't matter whether you're a main contractor or a developer; whether you're paying for goods or services. Subcontractors should charge the reduced VAT rate whenever possible.

Therefore contractors need to understand whether subcontractors have charged the correct rate of VAT. And, as I'll explain below, the rules are slightly different depending on whether we're dealing with qualifying conversions or renovations.

Qualifying conversions

In the case of qualifying new construction and conversions, the reduced rate applies to work carried out in the following circumstances:

- the work is carried out in the course of a new construction, qualifying conversion; and
- the services are "qualifying services".

This means that subcontractors are subject to the same rules as main contractors and can follow the rules explained in Chapters 11 and 12 and VAT Notice 708, sections 3 and 7. Subcontractors can charge the reduced rate for work done before completion, the same as the main contractor.

The main exception is where work is done on property used for "relevant charitable purposes" and "relevant residential purposes" – see below.

Qualifying renovations

The reduced rate for renovations applies in the circumstances explained in Chapter 12.

- The "first empty home test" applies when the property has been continuously empty (i.e. last lived in) during the two years before the contractor starts his work. If your services as a subcontractor are carried out before the property is occupied (under the "first empty home test"), the reduced rate can apply.

  However, if the *new owner* of the property moves in during the course of the renovation, then the first empty home test no longer applies. This means that services provided by both contractors AND subcontractors are standard rated.

- The "second empty home test" applies when the property is occupied but was empty for two years continuously before the current owner moved into the property AND the work is done for the new occupant/owner.

  In this situation, *the reduced rate only applies to services provided to the new home owner,* which means that sub-contractors' services are always standard rated because their services are supplied to the main contractor.

So ensure that your subcontractor is billing you at the correct rate.

Work on "certified" properties is always standard rated

Subcontractors must always charge VAT at 20% when working on a "certified building", i.e. if the property is for "relevant residential purposes"and "relevant charitable purposes". See VAT Notice 708, section 17.4 http://tinyurl.com/ndnm63g.

What if the contractor won't agree to charge VAT at the reduced rate but I'm sure that the work qualifies for the relief?

The contractor has to pay HMRC the correct amount of VAT on his sales. If he hasn't charged enough VAT, he is liable to pay it to HMRC even if he can't collect it from his customers. You can understand why contractors are cautious when deciding how much VAT to charge, otherwise they could be out of pocket.

If you think that the zero-rate or the reduced rate should apply more extensively, you could ask the builder to ask for a ruling from HMRC. Dealing with disagreements about the VAT liability of construction services should be covered in the contract to ensure that there is an agreed procedure for dealing with such situations.

At the end of the day, employing a contractor or sub-contractor is a commercial decision and VAT is part of that process. If you're particularly keen to use a particular builder or craftsman and they are unsure about the VAT, then perhaps you can agree to share the cost of asking HMRC for a ruling or asking a third party VAT consultant for an opinion.

Why worry if I can claim the VAT on my VAT returns

Are you sure you're entitled to claim the VAT?

- First of all, be certain that *your development qualifies for a refund*. You can normally only claim VAT if you're making taxable supplies; such as selling a property as a zero-rated supply, as explained in Chapter 8.
- Second, remember that *you can only claim VAT that has been correctly charged*. If you claim VAT on conversion work that qualified for the reduced rate of 5%, but you paid 20% VAT, HMRC will refuse to pay any of the claim because the invoice is invalid. If you've included such invoices on VAT returns, it means that the return is in error and you must ask the supplier to issue a credit note for the incorrect invoice and issue a correct invoice.   You must amend the original VAT return under the procedures explained in VAT Notice 700/45: How to correct VAT errors and make adjustments or claims http://tinyurl.com/clg48.

- Third reason is to *help with cash-flow*. Paying VAT at any stage can be a real drain on cash-flow. Even if you can claim VAT on your VAT returns, you have to allow a few weeks for the claim to be paid, especially in case HMRC decide to review the claim before paying.

Surely the best thing to do is to have the work done by contractors who aren't registered for VAT?

Using non-registered contractors is the only way to avoid VAT on labour costs. But what if the contractor also supplies goods or materials in the course of those services? In this case, you'll be paying 20% on all the goods and materials supplied by the contractor. The 20% cost on materials will be built into that quote from the unregistered contractor.

The examples below demonstrate the differences in cost depending on whether the contractor is registered for VAT. In each case, the charge for labour is £1,000 net of VAT. The examples show the difference based on goods that are less than the services, the same cost as the services or much higher than the services: £100, £1,000 and £10,000

Example 1: Cost of goods less than the services.

Unregistered contractor:

VAT inclusive goods: £120

Labour: £1,000

Total: £1,120.

Registered contractor: If he is registered for VAT, he can claim the £20 from HMRC but has to charge 5% VAT on the total net cost of the goods and services.

Net cost of goods: £100

Labour : £1000

Total net: £1,100 plus VAT @ 5% = £1,155

In this case, using a non-registered contractor can save **£35**

Example 2: Cost of goods and services are the same.

Unregistered contractor:

VAT inclusive goods: £1,200

Labour: £1,000

Total: £2,200

Registered contractor: If he is registered for VAT, he can claim the £200 from HMRC but has to charge 5% VAT on the total net cost of the goods and services.

Net cost of goods: £1,000

Labour : £1,000

Total net: £2,000 plus VAT @ 5% = £2,100

In this case, using a registered contractor can save **£100.**

Example 3: Cost of goods is significantly higher than the labour

Unregistered contractor:

VAT inclusive goods: £12,000

Labour: £1,000

Total: £13,000.

Registered contractor: If he is registered for VAT, he can claim the £20 from HMRC but has to charge 5% VAT on the total net cost of the goods and services.

Net cost of goods: £10,000

Labour : £1000

Total: £10,000 + £1,000 = £11,000@5% = £11,550.

In this case, the saving from using a registered contractor is proportionately much higher; i.e **£1,450**

So the potential saving depends on how much of the cost is for materials and how much for labour. **In practice, using an unregistered contractor is only cheaper if there's a higher proportion of labour to materials (whether it's bricks and mortar or new windows).** I'm sure that there is a mathematical formula that can work out the "tipping point" and quickly calculate when it's more cost effective to use a registered or non-registered contractor, but I'm no mathematician so I always end up doing the calculations on the back of an envelope using a calculator!

Either way, I'd suggest getting quotes from a number of contractors, including both registered and non-registered and see how the figures work out.

Either way, it's worth spending some time working out the figures to see which is the most cost effective way of engaging contractors.

But remember: *VAT is only one issue that you need to consider.* Over the years, I've seen many people get very bogged down in trying to save a few £100 VAT by employing the "cheapest" non-registered contractors or messing about asking a labour only contractor to buy goods at 20% and charge 5%. They may save a bit of money, but it's easy to lose sight of the big picture and end up with a lousy conversion or new dwelling. Don't engage a contractor who isn't registered for VAT just to save a bit of money if your gut is telling you to engage the VAT registered contractor.

I often hear this from both developers and contractors. And it important if you can't claim VAT because your sales are VAT exempt. However, the larger the conversion project you're doing, the more likely you are to engage a VAT registered contractor. They are normally more experienced and have the larger scale resources that you'll need to get your work done.

And you can sometimes save money by using a VAT registered contractor.

It all depends on the balance of "VAT free" labour and VAT bearing building materials. The higher the proportion of standard rated goods to labour, the more likely it will be that it will be cheaper to use a VAT registered contractor. This is because the contractor has to pay VAT at 20% on "builders'materials". If he is providing zero-rated or reduced rated services, he can claim the 20% VAT and charge you VAT at 5% for their supply and installation.

You might employ a mix of registered and non-registered contractors

You might decide to engage VAT registered businesses to carry out large value parts of the project which include large amounts of or expensive building materials, for example the bathroom or kitchen or infrastructure such as building walls, plumbing and gas/electricity – where you can benefit from the 5% rate. You can also engage self-employed decorators and other tradesmen who aren't registered for VAT for the labour intensive work such as decorating.

Of course this requires a bit more organisation and project management, but the VAT benefit could make the additional administration worthwhile. And you'll become more efficient managing such arrangements over time as you do more of these projects.

What if I'm a contractor and the client insists on paying in cash?

If a client insists on paying you in cash, you're still legally obliged to pay VAT on the amount of cash that you receive, whether it's liable to 20% or 5%. You treat the cash received as VAT inclusive. If the client insists on paying £10,000 then you'd calculate 20% VAT at $1/6^{th}$ and 5% VAT at $1/20^{st}$. If there is a mix of standard and reduced rate work, then you apportion the cost between the different elements and calculate $1/6^{th}$ and $1/20^{th.}$

If some or all of the work is eligible for the reduced rate, show them the calculations demonstrating how charging VAT could actually save them money.

Remember also that VAT registered contractors are required by law to issue a full VAT invoice (see appendix to Chapter 1) if the value of the work is more than £250.

Either way, whether you're a contractor or sub-contractor, or a specialist craftsman such as a wood restorer, make sure that you charge enough to cover your VAT liability so you're not left paying extra VAT to HMRC out of your own pocket.

Chapter 14: Checklist

- Subcontractors can charge the zero-rate or reduced rate if their services qualify.
- Main contractors can only recover VAT charged by subcontractors on building work if the VAT has been "correctly charged".
- Even if a customer pays you in cash, you still have to pay VAT to HMRC.
- It's usually cheaper to use unregistered contractors if they're only providing services.
- Depending on the proportion of labour to VAT bearing building materials, it's can be cheaper to use registered contractors for the provision and installation of goods to take advantage of the 5% reduced rate.

Chapter 15: Building materials

One of the most confusing areas of VAT and construction is the subject of "building materials". It causes more questions than just about any other specific topic, so you need to understand what it's all about.

- Goods and materials used in construction work
- What are building materials?
- How it works in practice: zero-rated new construction and reduced rated conversions and renovations
  - New construction
  - Renovations, conversions
- Goods that ARE NOT building materials
- Buying goods and materials from a supplier who doesn't install them

There are 2 very important aspects about this subject:

- whether the goods/materials qualify for the zero-rate or reduced rate; and
- whether you can claim VAT under the DIY refund scheme or if you're a VAT registered business.

I've explained the concept of "building materials" and when the zero-rate or reduced rate applies in this chapter.

Goods and materials used in construction work

As explained in previous chapters, the zero-rate and reduced rate applies to the construction of new dwellings and certain conversions and renovations AND *building materials used by the contractor in the course of the construction work.*

For example, if a contractor builds the walls of a new house, the zero-rate would apply to the labour and the bricks and mortar that he uses to build the walls. The goods on their own are always liable to 20% VAT - *it's when the goods are supplied with the building services that the zero-rate or reduced rate applies*.

However, this only applies if the goods and materials qualify as "building materials" for VAT purposes. So in

Goods and materials ONLY qualify for the zero-rate or reduced rate if they are "building materials" AND they are supplied by a contractor "in the course of" zero-rated new construction or reduced rated conversions or renovations.

this chapter, I'll explain what goods/materials ARE building materials and how the rule applies in practice.

N.B. *To avoid confusion, please note that the terms "supply" and "installation" normally refer to the sale of goods ("supply") and the labour cost of installing them ("installation"). In this chapter, I'll normally use the more everyday terms of goods (or "building materials") and labour.*

So what are building materials?

The VAT law says that the zero-rate and the reduced rate only apply to building materials that are incorporated into the new property in the course of the construction or conversion or renovation.

The basic criteria are as follows:

- The articles are incorporated into the buildings (or its site)
- the articles are "ordinarily" incorporated by builders into that type of building
- other than kitchen furniture, the articles are not finished or prefabricated furniture, or materials for the construction of fitted furniture
- with certain exceptions, the articles are not gas or electrical appliances
- the articles are not carpets or carpeting material

THE GOODS MUST MEET <u>ALL</u> OF THESE RULES TO QUALIFY AS BUILDING MATERIALS.

Some people think that the rule means that you can't save VAT on "luxury" expenditure and that HMRC deliberately applies the rules very strictly. However the rules are part of the law, which means that HMRC have to apply the rules correctly.

HMRC's guidance on this subject is in VAT Notice 708, paragraph 13 http://tinyurl.com/mohugtx.

It contains lists of goods that qualify as "building materials" in VAT Notice 708: Buildings and construction, paragraph 13: http://tinyurl.com/gp44w8s.

As you'll see, their list is quite detailed, but like all guidance, it can't possibly cover every possible type of expenditure.

I've also discussed some of the more commonly asked questions in more detail in <u>Chapter 21</u>: FAQs, to help point you in the right direction.

How it works in practice: zero-rated new construction and reduced rated conversions and renovations

So how do the rules work in practice? The rules are slightly different for zero-rated new construction and reduced rated conversions and renovations.

For example, let's consider how the rule applies to two different products; an electrical boiler which heats the building's water and an integrated oven which doesn't heat water or the room, but only cooks food.

Usually, electrical appliances are NOT regarded as building materials - see the 4th bullet point in the list on the previous page. However, if you look in VAT Notice 708, paragraph 16.6, you'll see a list of the gas and electrical appliances that ARE regarded as building materials. This includes goods which are:

"designed by the manufacturers to heat space or water (this includes cookers which are designed to have a dual purpose to heat the room or the building's water)".

Boilers are designed to heat water, so the boiler qualifies as a building material.
However, integrated ovens that only cook food ARE NOT building materials.

So how does this affect the VAT liability of the goods themselves and the contractors' services of installing the goods?

As you'll see below, the rules are slightly different depending on whether we're looking at zero-rated new construction or reduced rated conversions and renovations.

New construction

The contractor can zero-rate the services of installing a boiler and the boiler itself.

The contractor has to charge VAT at 20% on the amount charged for the oven *but can zero-rate the charge for installing the oven as long as this is done in the course of construction of the new dwelling.* *

Conversion and renovations

The contractor can charge the reduced rate for the services of installing the boiler and the boiler itself.

The contractor has to charge 20% VAT for the oven *and must also charge 20% for installing the oven.* *

See VAT Notice 708, paragraph 18.2: http://tinyurl.com/gp44w8s

*The difference between new construction and reduced rated conversions/renovations is how VAT applies to the labour (i.e. installation) service if the goods ARE NOT building materials. The contractor can zero-rate the installation charge in new construction even if the goods are NOT building materials. However the reduced rate for the installation of goods in reduced rated conversions/renovations ONLY applies if the goods themselves are building materials.

See Chapters 17 - 20 for more information about when developers can claim VAT.

Goods that aren't building materials

The supply of, or supply and installation of goods that aren't building materials is normally standard rated. Some of the best known examples are fitted furniture (other than kitchen units) and most kitchen appliances.

Buying goods and materials from a supplier who doesn't install them

If you buy goods direct from a supplier who DOESN'T install them, then you'll pay 20% VAT, whether or not the goods are "building materials". You can only claim this VAT if the goods are "building materials" and they are installed into the building in the course of construction or conversion. If you don't use the goods in the new/converted property and sell them separately, then you have to charge 20% VAT.

Chapter 15: Checklist

- Goods used in new construction, conversions and renovations are normally called "building materials".
- The term "building materials" is defined in the legislation.
- The criteria are detailed and strictly enforced by HMRC.
- The zero-rate or reduced rate applies to building materials supplied by and incorporated into the property in the course of the zero-rated or reduced rated construction work.
- If the goods are not "building materials", the contractor must charge 20% VAT for those goods.
- In new construction, even if the goods are not "building materials", the contractor can zero-rate the installation (i.e. the labour element) of those goods in the course of construction of the new dwelling.
- In reduced rated renovations and conversions, if the goods are not "building materials", the contractor has to charge VAT at 20% for installing (i.e. the labour element) the goods.
- If you buy goods directly, you have to pay 20% VAT. You can only claim this VAT if you're entitled to claim under the DIY refund scheme and the goods themselves would be "building materials" if supplied and installed by a contractor.

Chapter 16

VAT savings on other types of construction work

In this chapter, we'll look at the VAT liability of other types of construction work carried out on existing properties and when it might be possible to save VAT by taking advantage of other reliefs.

- Redecoration, alterations, repairs and maintenance ("RAR&M") work
- Installation of energy saving insulation
- Installation of grant funded heating
- Adaptations for the handicapped
- Adaptations for the elderly

> If the main conversion or renovation work doesn't qualify for the reduced rate in its own right, then you may still be able to save on VAT expenditure if any of the work falls within the categories mentioned below.

The reliefs explained in this chapter are limited. They fall into 2 main categories: first, reliefs for the elderly and the disabled; second the reduced rate in respect of certain supplies of environmentally friendly energy and heating measures. They are each explained in detail in various HMRC publications or specific pages on the HMRC website, with the relevant links shown below.

As always, I'd recommend that you read the information below in conjunction with HMRC's guidance to get the full picture. The information is spread over several different places on HMRC's website, with links as shown below.

Redecoration, alterations, repairs and maintenance work ("RARM")

In principle, unless the work is carried out as part of a qualifying conversion or renovation, RARM is all standard rated.

Renovations and conversions are also standard rated, _unless the work qualifies under the rules explained in Chapter 12._ So if, for example, you're renovating a house which has been empty for 18 months, the renovation is standard rated. If you're converting an old pub which has an existing self-contained flat into a single house, the conversion is standard rated.

So you have to budget for VAT at 20% on conversion work in these situations. And the VAT can't be claimed, even if you're planning to sell the property, because the completed property isn't a "converted non-residential property" as explained in Chapter 8. You'll need to budget for the irclaimable VAT at the planning stage, especially if you're applying for a bank loan to fund the project.

Other reduced rate and zero-rated work.

Installation of certain energy-saving materials is eligible for the reduced rate of VAT

Information about this relief is in HMRC VAT Notice 708/6: Energy-saving materials
http://tinyurl.com/brtzhub.

- The reduced rate applies when the materials are installed in residential accommodation, including dwellings and multi-occupancy buildings; or when the properties are used by charities for non-business purposes.
- The notice lists the materials that are covered by the relief (see section 2.5). They include such things as insulation; controls for heating and water systems; solar panels; wind or water turbines.
- The notice also clarifies when certain other services that are ancillary to the installation of the energy-saving materials are covered by the reduced rate, such as extending the size of a loft hatch to enable access to lofts when installing insulation.
- Insulation of whole central heating systems is not covered by the reduced rate, unless under the grant funded scheme mentioned below.

HMRC's notice also explains HMRC's view about the VAT liability of installation of the energy-saving materials done at the same time as other construction work, such as extending a property to create an additional dwelling. In some cases, the installation of the energy-saving materials would be regarded as a mixed supply, which can be apportioned between standard rated and reduced rate work as explained in Chapter 1.

Installation of grant funded heating system measures is eligible for the reduced rate of VAT

The intention of this relief is to help those on lower incomes install certain heating measures in their homes.

The main principles are similar to those applying to the installation of energy-saving materials, as explained above, with the following differences:

- It only applies to the supply and installation of such equipment that are funded by grants, such as grants from local authorities.

- The recipient must fall within the definition of a "qualifying person"; including the over 60's and those receiving certain types of benefit.
- It can apply to the installation of a wide range of heating equipment including central heating, storage heaters, radiators, gas-fired boilers. A full list is included in section 3 of Notice 708/6.

The reduced rate also applies to grant-funded connection or reconnection to a mains gas supply relating to a qualifying person's sole or main residence.

Alterations to suit the condition of people with disabilities is eligible for the zero-rate

Certain alteration work for people with disabilities can be zero-rated. The work covered by the includes:

- Constructing a ramp or widening a doorway or passage.
- Providing, extending or adapting a bathroom, toilet or washroom.

The zero-rate only applies when the work and related goods is done at the person's home; certain charitable buildings and residential homes. The customer has to provide a certificate confirming that he/she is eligible for the relief.

Further details can be found in HMRC VAT Notice 701/7: VAT Reliefs for Disabled People, section 6 **http://tinyurl.com/btkcskn.** Details of the certificates that are required are at section 10 of the notice.

Installation of mobility aids for the elderly for use in domestic accommodation is eligible for the reduced rate

The reduced rate applies to certain installation of mobility aids for the elderly in domestic accommodation, as explained here:
http://www.hmrc.gov.uk/vat/sectors/consumers/mobility-aids.htm

People aged 60 or over are entitled to the reduced rate of VAT on the supply and installation of these items:

- grab rails
- ramps
- stair lifts

- bath lifts
- built-in shower seats or showers containing built-in shower seats
- walk-in baths with sealable doors

The guidance explains that the relief only applies when the goods are installed in private homes. The customer has to provide a certificate to the contractor confirming his/her eligibility for the reduced rate. The certificate is contained in the HMRC guidance.

Chapter 16: Checklist

- Redecoration, alterations, repairs and maintenance ("RAR&M") work carried out in the course of qualifying conversions and renovations normally qualifies for the reduced rate.
- Other RARM work is liable to VAT at 20%.
- Installation of certain energy saving insulation and grant funded heating systems is eligible for the reduced rate.
- Certain domestic adaptations for the handicapped and the elderly are zero-rated if the customer provides a certificate confirming that they are eligible for the relief.

The 3 step process: Step 3

Claiming VAT on costs

Chapter 17: Being a VAT registered business

Before you can claim any VAT on conversions from HMRC, you have to be registered for VAT.

This chapter is for those of you going into business for the first time who may have to register for VAT, particularly those of you planning to sell new or converted non-residential properties as discussed in Chapter 8.

- VAT registration for property businesses
- How and when to register for VAT
  - When you are liable to register
  - When the registration starts
  - How and when do I have to notify HMRC that I'm liable to register?
- Other types of VAT registration
  - Voluntary registration when turnover is below the registration limit
  - Registering to claim VAT on expenditure
  - Registering before making any sales
  - Group registration for associated companies
  - Exemption from registration when VAT on expenditure exceeds VAT on sales
- Registration for property businesses: Form V5
- What if my sales are zero-rated and all I want to do is to claim VAT on my expenditure from HMRC?
  - Monthly VAT returns
- Claiming VAT on pre-registration expenditure
- Being VAT registered
  - Paying VAT on other income
  - Closely linked businesses
- Cancelling your registration
  - Claiming VAT on expenditure incurred after deregistration: VAT 427
- Keeping records and accounts
- Find a good accountant!

HMRC VAT Notice 700/1: Should I be registered for VAT? http://tinyurl.com/lvomafd explains the issues discussed in this chapter in much more detail. I've included links to the most important sections.

VAT registration for property businesses

In Chapter 4, I explained that you have to register for VAT if your activities are "in the course or furtherance of a business" and the value of your taxable sales exceeds the VAT registration limit.

The definition of "the course or furtherance of a business" applies to a wide range of activities, including not-for-profit transactions, sales of goods by charities and even certain transactions that aren't "sales" in the normal sense of the word. These include the use of business assets for personal purposes, such as petrol in company cars, or using an office computer for your personal emails or web-browsing.

It can also include the sale of a single property done in the course or furtherance of a business. This often brings people into the VAT registration "club" for the first time. For example, you might convert a non-residential property into a couple of dwellings and you plan to live in one and sell the other. Your income from the sale would be regarded as a business activity and if the value of the zero-rated sale exceeds the VAT registration limit (£85,000 in May 2017) you are REQUIRED to notify HMRC that you're liable to register.

If the development is a one-time event, never to be repeated, then the law allows HMRC to disregard the sale so that you don't have to register if you don't want to. However even in this situation, you MUST notify HMRC that you're liable to register. In practice, developers usually WANT to register to claim VAT on their costs if the sale is zero-rated as explained in Chapter 8.

You might also receive "taxable" income from dwellings used as holiday lets, which is liable to VAT at 20%. This subject is covered in more detail in Chapter 9.

*Limit correct at date of publication, but please check the HMRC website for future registration limit and VAT Notice 701/1, section 2 for historic thresholds: http://tinyurl.com/gwfby99.

How and when should I register for VAT?

When you become liable to register

The actual date on which you register for VAT depends on the specific circumstances of your business, as I'll explain below.

The process of registering for VAT includes two separate and distinct steps: the first is NOTIFYING HMRC THAT YOU'RE LIABLE TO REGISTER to register for VAT; the second is BECOMING REGISTERED for VAT; as explained below.

Step 1: You have to NOTIFY HMRC THAT YOU'RE LIABLE TO REGISTER within certain time limits as explained below. You may have to pay a penalty if you don't do this at the right time. Notifying is normally done by submitting the application form VAT 1 http://tinyurl.com/8l8ejcj

WHEN do I have to notify HMRC?

The notification requirement means that you have to NOTIFY HMRC when you are liable to register for VAT. This is normally as follows:

- You must notify HMRC that you're liable to register within thirty days of the date on which the value of your taxable sales has exceeded the VAT registration limit, i.e. £85,000 in the previous twelve months; OR
- At any time when you know that the value of your taxable sales will exceed the registration limit in the next thirty days.

Step 2: WHEN THE REGISTRATION COMMENCES: This will depend on your specific situation, but if you're already trading and the value of your sales has already exceeded the registration limit at the end of any 12 month period, then you'll be registered from the first day of the second month after the end of the 12 month period.

Example If your income in the twelve months to 31 March was £85,000 then you'd have to notify HMRC that you're liable to register by the end of the following month; 30 April. Your registration would take effect on 1 May.

Otherwise, you can apply to register from an earlier date as explained below.

HOW do I notify HMRC?

You have to notify HMRC by submitting an application to register for VAT, form VAT 1 which is submitted electronically.

Further guidance about the process is at section 4 of Notice 700/1 http://tinyurl.com/nyvwvku.

There are penalties for failing to notify that you're liable to register for VAT at the right time, so that's why it's important to make the application at the right time. The penalties wouldn't normally apply if your only business activity is the zero-rated sale of the converted dwelling (other than a £50 minimum fine), but it's a good idea to start your VAT relationship with HMRC in the right way by submitting your application at the right time.

Other types of registration

Voluntary registration: if your turnover below registration limits

You can also register for VAT on a voluntary basis if your turnover isn't above the limits – see Notice 700/1 section 3.9 http://tinyurl.com/nyvwvku.

Registering BEFORE you make any sales: "intending trader"

You can apply to register BEFORE you make any sales to enable you to claim VAT on your expenditure as you go along, as an **"intending trader"**. In this scenario, you're registering because you INTEND to make taxable sales at a later date, as explained at section 3.9 of Notice 700/1.

If you apply to register as an intending trader, you have to prove that you're planning to "make taxable sales" to HMRC, usually by providing evidence such as planning permissions, purchase invoices, contracts etc.

The "intending trader" registration is ideal if you're building new dwellings or converting a non-residential property to sell.

It means you can claim VAT on your purchases and expenses while you're in the course of carrying out your property build or conversion, even if you don't have a prospective buyer lined up. It's particularly useful to help with cash-flow if you're on a very tight budget. You also can ask HMRC to allow you to submit monthly VAT returns to enable you to get those VAT repayments as soon as possible while you're busy building or converting the property.

Exemption from registration when VAT on expenditure exceeds VAT on sales

You can be granted "exemption from registration" if the VAT on your expenditure would always be more than the VAT on your sales. A good example would be a butcher selling fresh meat, whose sales are mostly zero-rated and whose only input tax is on the expenditure of running the shop itself – utilities, phone bill etc.

In those circumstances the business owner can ask to be "exempt from registration" as explained in Notice 700/1, section 3.11 http://tinyurl.com/nyvwvku. You'd still have to submit an application to register under the normal rules, but you check the section on the VAT registration form which asks if you want to be exempted from registration.

Group registration for associated companies

Associated companies are able to register for VAT as a VAT group. This can make life a lot easier because it means that group members don't have to issue invoices for sales of goods and services between themselves. The group nominates a "representative member" who submits a single VAT return on behalf of the group as a whole.

Most large corporate groups use this facility nowadays. However it's not always the best way of organizing VAT affairs for property groups, especially if any of the companies makes "exempt supplies" and is partly exempt (i.e. receives income from exempt residential lets – see Chapter 18).

There are also several anti-avoidance provisions that apply to large businesses, particularly corporate groups; including certain transactions involving property and certain international services. Large commercial property developers who operate as part of a corporate group are probably affected by one or more of these provisions. Residential property developers in that situation will almost certainly need tailored VAT advice.

****

The subject of VAT registration can be complicated and different procedures apply in different situations. I've only been able to cover the most common in this chapter, but there are other factors to consider which are explained in Notice 700/1 http://tinyurl.com/lvomafd.

The officers at HMRC's VAT registration offices are usually very helpful if you have any queries about making the application and whether or not you need to register for VAT.

Registration for property businesses: Form V5

HMRC have introduced an additional step into the VAT registration process for property related businesses, to provide HMRC with more detailed information about the type of property business and to help them identify the nature of the business's income and expenditure. Form V5 http://tinyurl.com/kggq8hy is to be completed online as part of the registration process. It's a fairly straightforward process, taking business owners through a simple questionnaire about their business activities. It enables HMRC to make sure that each business is allocated to the right trade/risk category for their administration purposes.

What if my sales are zero-rated and all I want to do is to claim VAT on my expenditure from HMRC?

If the sale of your property qualifies for zero-rating under the rules explained in the Chapter 12, then you can register for VAT and claim VAT on the related expenditure. For many of you, this will be the only reason that you register for VAT. Such businesses are normally called "repayment traders".

But remember that once you're registered for VAT, you have to follow the same rules that apply to other VAT registered businesses – it's not a case of picking and choosing the bits that apply to you.

Monthly VAT returns

If you're a repayment trader, then you can ask HMRC for permission to submit monthly VAT returns to help with your cash-flow. This is particularly helpful for property developers because funding the VAT element of construction services, whether at 20% or even at 5%, can be a real drain on cash-flow.

If you're submitting repayment claims on a regular basis, HMRC will almost certainly want to inspect your records so make sure that everything is up to date and available for inspection

To speed up the process, you can always send copies of the invoices to your local VAT office at the same time that the return is submitted so that they have the documentation to hand to validate your claim.

HMRC has to pay VAT claims within certain time limits or risk having to pay a supplement of 5% to the claimant.

You can normally stay on monthly returns indefinitely. However as and when your circumstances change and you start making payment returns – perhaps you start receiving VAT on rent for opted commercial property lettings or holiday lets – you can ask to change to quarterly returns.

HMRC will normally allow you to choose your preferred quarter end (referred to as the "stagger"). You can benefit from choosing the stagger which gives you most cash-flow advantage for your rental income. For example, if you've opted to tax a commercial property and your tenants pay rent on the normal calendar quarterly days, the VAT return stagger of February, May, August and November will enable you to benefit from having the VAT on the rent in your bank account for more than three months before you have to pay the VAT to HMRC.

Claiming VAT on pre-registration expenses

If you don't want to register until you start generating taxable income, you can normally claim VAT on cost incurred before the registration that are used to make taxable supplies after registration as follows:

- Goods and materials – up to four years prior to registration if they are still on hand at the date of registration; and
- Services incurred in the six months prior to registration.

In either case, remember that <u>you can only claim VAT on goods and services used to make taxable supplies after you've registered for VAT</u>. You CANNOT claim any VAT on costs used to make exempt supplies after registration.

See VAT Notice 700, section 11 http://tinyurl.com/ngmnkzz for further information about pre-registration input tax.

For example you might be doing a relatively simple non-residential conversion project which will only take two or three months to complete. You intend to sell the converted properties on completion. You don't want the hassle of submitting monthly VAT returns during the conversion process, preferring to submit one single repayment claim return once the property has been sold.

Alternatively, perhaps your original intention was to retain the property as an investment property to generate rental income, but you get an offer to purchase the properties once they've been completed, generating income from zero-rated sales. In this situation, you can register for VAT and claim VAT on the cost of the conversion under the pre-registration rules.

Either way, make sure that you check out the rules in some detail – especially if you have income from other business activities that could be affected by registering for VAT.

Being registered for VAT

Once you've registered for VAT, this is what you have to do:

- Keep records and accounts up to date.

- Submit VAT returns.

- Pay VAT on any other income that is liable to VAT at 20% and/or 5%.

- Claim VAT on goods and services used to make taxable sales; i.e. those at 20%, 5% or the zero-rate.

There's a lot of guidance on the HMRC website for newly registered businesses. The best place to start is their "VAT Guide", VAT Notice 700 http://tinyurl.com/9ykqw which contains detailed guidance about most VAT issues. It's over 200 pages long, but you probably only need to read certain parts. You may prefer to start with HMRC's "Ins and Outs of VAT", 700/15 http://tinyurl.com/33crxs5.

If you have a good accountant they should be able to do your VAT returns and help you deal with your day to day VAT issues. But it is your responsibility to get you VAT affairs right so don't assume that they can deal with every specific VAT issue for you. They may have clients from a wide range of business sectors and VAT is only one of the subjects they're expected to deal with every day.

Paying VAT on other income

Once you have registered for VAT, you have to pay VAT on all of your taxable (i.e. liable to VAT) business income. Remember *it's the business owner who is registered for VAT*, so whether it's a limited company, a partnership or sole proprietor, the registration covers all of the owner's activities.

And if you choose to register for VAT as an "intending trader", you have to pay VAT on any taxable income that you receive after you register, even if you're still months away from completing your property conversion.

Example

Suppose you're a building contractor and you've purchased a property to convert into a dwelling and sell. Your contracting income has always been below the VAT registration limit. If you register for VAT, you'd also have to pay VAT on all your contracting income. This means that you add VAT at 5% or 20% to your invoices, or alternatively pay $1/21^{st}$ or $1/6^{th}$ out of your income as VAT, treating your income as VAT inclusive as explained in the appendix to Chapter 1.

Income from other "closely linked" businesses
Disaggregation or "artificial splitting of businesses".

Suppose our VAT registered building contractor set up a separate limited company for the conversion business to keep the finances separate from their construction business. The income from the conversion business is below the VAT registration limit.

The law also allows HMRC to treat all of the income in the above situations as though received by one party, either you or the company which means that you would have to pay VAT on all of the income.

And it can also apply to income from other non-registered business to which you are linked, for example your spouse's income from their business.

> The principle can apply whenever having separate businesses or different legal entities gives rise to a VAT advantage. It can apply even if the VAT advantage isn't even INTENTIONAL, so there's no onus on HMRC to prove that the motive for separate businesses is to save VAT.

To minimize the risk that HMRC would regard your arrangements as "artificial splitting of businesses", take sensible practical steps such as keeping separate proper records and accounts for each business, use separate premises and make sure that you charge for the provision of goods or services between the separate businesses at the normal market rate.

HMRC provide guidance explaining when they WOULD apply the rule and when they would not apply the rule: http://tinyurl.com/n9y6qmh.

Cancelling your registration

You can ask to HMRC to cancel your registration if your turnover drops below the "deregistration limit" which is currently £83,000 excluding VAT (May 2017). You MUST cancel your registration if you stop trading altogether. The "deregistration limit" is normally raised in line with inflation each year. Further information on when and how to deregister is in VAT Notice 700/11: Cancelling your registration http://tinyurl.com/p5cpjb3.

Section 9 of the Notice explains when and you can claim VAT on expenditure incurred after registration that related to your VAT registered business by using form VAT 427 http://tinyurl.com/q7hurva.

Keeping records and accounts

Once you register for VAT, you must keep your records and accounts up to date. In practice these usually means maintaining normal accounting records. You also have to prepare a "VAT account", which is a summary of the VAT on your sales and purchases that you prepare each time you complete your VAT return. See HMRC's general guidance here http://tinyurl.com/phhscnq and VAT Notice 700/20 http://tinyurl.com/opqouor.

It's particularly important to keep accurate records up to date, especially if you have both taxable and exempt income and have to allocate your costs to either type of income for partial exemption purposes, as explained in Chapter 18.

First time business? Find a good accountant or book-keeper

For some of you, getting into property conversions and renovations might be your first foray into being self-employed and running your own business. You may be reading this book as one of your first pieces of research in advance of buying your first property for conversion.

One of the most important things is to FIND A GOOD ACCOUNTANT OR BOOK-KEEPER. There are thousands of accountants and book-keepers out there who provide services to small business owners and market themselves as specialising in new businesses. Some are better than others and it's worth investing in a good one.

And of course, going into property development is one of the most complex areas of the VAT law so you'll need an accountant who is experienced with VAT issues. **However, please don't expect your accountant to understand all of the detailed VAT rules explained in this book.** Most accountants are really good at doing VAT returns and dealing with day to day practical VAT issues. However, it isn't fair to expect them to deal with the more complex VAT issues explained in this book. That's when you have to do your own homework by reading up on the subject or take professional advice from a professional VAT consultant if you need help.

Chapter 17: Checklist

- You must register for VAT if your taxable income from any business exceeds the VAT registration limit, currently £85,000 per 12 month period or you anticipate your turnover will exceed the registration limit in the following <u>30 days</u>.
- You can't register if your only income is VAT exempt; e.g. short term residential lettings.
- You can register if your only sales are zero-rated to claim VAT on expenditure.
- You have to notify HMRC that you're liable to register within certain time limits.
- You have to apply to register online using form VAT 1.
- Property and construction businesses also have to submit form VAT 5L to give HMRC information about their business activities.
- You can register before you make any sales to claim VAT on your expenditure in advance.
- Being VAT registered means you have to pay VAT on all of your income and possibly income from other related businesses.
- You have to keep records and accounts up to date, especially if you have income from both taxable and exempt sales or rents.
- Invest in a good accountant or book-keeper.

Chapter 18

Introduction: when VAT registered property converters can claim VAT

The rules for claiming VAT on costs are explained in detail in VAT Notice 700: The VAT Guide, sections 10 - 13 http://tinyurl.com/naph8nq.

Blocked input tax

One of the main rules is that regardless of your business activity and the VAT liability of your income, you CAN'T claim VAT on certain costs, which includes expenditure such as business entertainment or buying a car - see VAT Notice 700, section 10.3 http://tinyurl.com/kk92jgg. This VAT is referred to as "blocked input tax".

I've explained the main rules about claiming VAT from HMRC for those of you make both taxable and exempt supplies in this chapter, with some further information on some more complex issues in Chapters 19 and 20.

HMRC VAT Notices:

VAT Notice 700: The VAT Guide, sections 10 – 13 http://tinyurl.com/naph8nq

VAT Notice 706: Partial Exemption: http://tinyurl.com/6q67c38 also includes guidance about the clawback and payback rules which I'll explain in Part 3 of this chapter.

Notice 706/2: The Capital Goods Scheme explains how the CGS works http://tinyurl.com/3vvf4b4.

VAT registered property developers: claiming VAT on costs
Introduction to partial exemption

> Partial exemption is the term used to describe the situation when businesses make both taxable and exempt sales AND incur VAT on expenditure relating to both classes of income.

Basic principles

The basic principles about claiming VAT are very logical. You can claim VAT relating to taxable income as input tax on your VAT return, but you can't claim normally VAT on costs relating to exempt income (i.e. "exempt input tax"). Businesses that have both taxable and exempt income are known as "partly exempt" businesses

- Partial exemption rules
- Calculating how much VAT you can claim
- The standard method
  - Income that can be excluded
  - The partial exemption year
  - Annual adjustments
  - "De minimis" limits
  - Example: Residual input tax and annual adjustments
- Special partial exemption methods
- Record keeping

Property developers make supplies that are both taxable and exempt. They must follow the partial exemption principles to work out how much VAT on cost they can claim from HMRC.

Partial exemption rules

The principles of VAT recovery (i.e. how much you can claim from HMRC) are relatively simple but can be difficult to apply in practice. HMRC's detailed guidance about VAT recovery is in VAT Notice 706: Partial Exemption: http://tinyurl.com/lst93y9. I've included several links to relevant sections for your reference in Chapter 19.

One of the reasons the subject of VAT recovery is so confusing is the terminology. It's all about attribution, fractions, apportionment - nothing that's very tangible. If you think about VAT on income and contractor's services can be a bit difficult, at least they deal with practical issues of construction services and selling or letting property.

Calculating how much VAT you can claim, however, is based on a series of principles and calculations and attributions, so it can be much more difficult to get your head around the subject. Some of it sounds like a different language.

That's why it's important to get your head round the main principles.

Business/non-business costs

The very first stage is to calculate any VAT on costs of goods and services used for non-business activities, such as personal use or charitable use. Check out VAT Notice 700, the VAT Guide, section 4.6.3 http://tinyurl.com/njqq9k3 for information about non-business activities.

You can't claim ANY VAT on goods or services used for non-business activities.

Direct attribution

The next step is identifying whether goods or services are used or will be used to make taxable or exempt supplies. This first step is "direct attribution" where you identify goods and services used wholly to make either taxable or exempt supplies; e.g. zero-rate sales or exempt rental income.

- You can claim VAT on costs used wholly to make taxable supplies.
- VAT on costs used wholly to make exempt supplies is called "exempt input tax".
- Costs that are used to make both types of supply, e.g. office overhead costs, accountancy fees, fuel costs, are called "residual" costs and the VAT is apportioned between taxable supplies and exempt supplies. The standard method used to attribute this VAT between taxable and exempt supplies is the partial exemption "method" as explained below.
- If the total "exempt input tax" i.e. directly attributable and proportion of residual VAT is within the "de minimis" limit, you can claim all of the VAT. Otherwise, you can't claim ANY exempt input tax.

The procedure is shown step by step in the box later in this chapter.

The standard partial exemption method

The "standard method" is the normal way of calculating how much of your residual VAT is attributable to your taxable sales. It is the method defined in the VAT legislation. You have to use this method unless HMRC have agreed that you can use a "special method" as explained below.

Under the standard method, your residual input tax is apportioned between your taxable and exempt sales by reference to the proportion that taxable income bears to total income in that VAT period. More information is in VAT Notice 706, section 4 http://tinyurl.com/q5co7c2..

Standard method: income you can exclude

If you're using the "standard method", you can normally exclude the values of certain transactions because they will distort the calculation. This includes the sale of capital assets and real estate and financial transactions, such as bank interest, that are incidental to your main business activity. More information on this is in VAT Notice 706, section 4.8: http://tinyurl.com/q5co7c2.

Whether or not such transactions are distortive depends on the type of transaction and business. For example, income from the occasional sale of a property by a manufacturing company would probably be regarded as distortive. However the value of a zero-rated sale of a converted non-residential property by a residential landlord might be regarded as distortive. Including the value of the sale in the standard method calculation may enable the business to claim VAT that relates to its exempt residential letting because it inflates the value of taxable supplies. Each situation has to be considered on its own merits.

Calculating how much VAT you can claim

Main partial exemption principles

1. First, identify expenditure which relate wholly to either taxable or exempt supplies made by the business, whether in that VAT return period or in the future. This is called "direct attribution" and should be used as far as possible to allocate expenditure to income.

2. VAT on expenditure that is directly attributed to taxable sales can be claimed in full (subject to the exceptions listed on page 161).

3. VAT on expenditure that is directly attributed to exempt supplies is called "exempt input tax" and can only be claimed if the total exempt input tax is below the "de minimis" limit.

4. Expenditure that can't be directly attributed to any particular business income – such as overhead expenditure – are called "residual". VAT on these costs is called "residual input tax".

5. Residual input tax is then apportioned between taxable and exempt supplies in the same proportion as the value of taxable sales bears to the total supplies made in that VAT period. This is called the **STANDARD METHOD**. Other allocation methods can be used, but normally only with agreement from HMRC. These are called **SPECIAL METHODS**.

6. For example: if 60% of the business's income in that period is taxable income and 40% is exempt, then 60% of the residual input tax can be claimed as it is attributable to taxable supplies.

7. The remaining 40% is "exempt input tax".

8. The total "exempt input tax" is the total directly attributed exempt input tax from step 3 plus the proportion of the residual input tax calculated at step 5. It can only be claimed if it falls within the "de minimis" limit which is currently £7,500 (i.e. £625 per month) and less than 50% of all input tax in the partial exemption year concerned.

9. An annual adjustment is carried out at the end of each VAT year to balance seasonal fluctuations.

The standard method is a very simple way of calculating recoverable VAT, but it can sometimes produce distortive results depending on when large value transactions and related expenditure occur. I've given an example below showing how VAT recovery can be significantly affected by the timing of transactions.

The partial exemption year

The "partial exemption year" or "VAT year" normally runs from 1 April, 1 May or 1 June to the following 31 March, 30 April or 31 May according to the businesses' VAT return periods. You can ask HMRC to use a different year – perhaps a calendar year – to fit in with annual accounts or for other reasons.

Annual adjustments

Initial partial exemption calculations are made in each VAT quarter. These are provisional calculations and businesses carry out an adjustment each year to balance out fluctuations. This is called the "annual adjustment". It's made at the end of each "partial exemption year", which runs in tandem with the business's VAT quarters, starting on 1 April, 1 May or 1 June each year.

See VAT Notice 706, section 12: http://tinyurl.com/pgh2fol for more information about annual adjustments.

N.B. There are special partial exemption accounting periods for businesses who "become partly exempt"; i.e. you start to incur expenditure relating to exempt supplies for the first time. These are called "longer periods". There are also special accounting periods for newly registered businesses and businesses which are de-registering. See VAT Notice 706, section 12.3 for more information: http://tinyurl.com/p7ryurf.

"De minimis" limits

The "de minimis" limit is £7,500 (i.e. £625 per month) and less than 50% of all input tax in the partial exemption year concerned. If you're looking at individual VAT quarters, then the limit is £1,875 and 50% of input tax in that VAT period.

See VAT Notice 706, section 11: http://tinyurl.com/czhj6to for more information about the partial exemption de minimis limit.

How does it work in practice?

Suppose you build 2 houses, paying £20,000 VAT on over the 12 month period, while the VAT on costs relating to a couple of rental properties is £1,000. In that case, you could claim all of the VAT because the exempt input tax falls within the "de minimis" limit.

However, suppose you've done a large renovation of the rental property, costing £50,000 and £10,000 VAT. In that case, the exempt input tax of £10,000 exceeds the "de minimis" limit so you can't claim it back.

Case study

- For example, let's consider the developer in our case study. The developer paid £11,200 VAT on costs to convert his property into 2 flats, which are leased on exempt short term residential leases. The £11,200 is exempt input tax and exceeds the "de minimis" limit, so the developer can't claim any of this VAT.
- However if the developer grants a 99 year lease in one of the flats, then the sale would be zero-rated. Therefore the developer can claim the VAT on related costs because the costs are directly attributable to the zero-rated sale; i.e. £5,600.
- And because the remaining exempt input tax is now reduced to £5,600, the developer can also claim this VAT because it falls within the "de minimis" limit of £7,500 per VAT year and 50% of all input tax.

There are several detailed aspects to the rules, such as how to apportion overhead costs between taxable and exempt income, annual adjustments and other adjustment rules that are explained in the next chapter. If you're a property developer, you will probably need to spend some time learning how these rules work in more detail.

Partial Exemption Special Methods

If the standard method based on turnover is not "fair and reasonable", HMRC can also allow or direct businesses to use special partial exemption methods. HMRC's guidance is in VAT Notice 706, section 6: http://tinyurl.com/oyg393k. See Chapter 20 where I've discussed the subject of partial exemption for house-builders for more information.

Record keeping

At the risk of repeating myself again and again, I can't stress enough how important it is to keep accurate records of expenditure and whether it relates to your taxable income (zero-rated sales; standard rated holiday lets) or exempt income (e.g. short term residential lets). You also need to keep proper records of income.

In practice, your normal record-keeping should be enough to provide the information you need to work out your VAT returns. But have a word with your accountant or book-keeper if you think that you may need any further information for VAT purposes.

Chapter 18: Checklist

- If you have income from both taxable and exempt supplies, your business is "partly exempt" for VAT purposes.
- Under the law, you have to identify expenditure that is directly attributable to either taxable or exempt supplies.
- VAT that can't be attributed to either class of supply is "residual input tax" and should be apportioned between taxable and exempt under a partial exemption method.
- The normal method is based on income, but you can apply to HMRC to use a "special method".
- You make provisional partial exemption calculations each VAT quarter, with annual adjustments for each VAT year.
- You have to ensure that your expenditure is properly allocated to income in your accounting records and that the records are kept up to date.

Chapter 19

When things don't go to plan: Adjusting VAT claims in future years

"Clawback/payback" and the Capital goods scheme

The partial exemption rules can be particularly difficult for property developers for several reasons. One of the most difficult is dealing with income and expenditure that occur over a number of years, which is typical for property developers. Also, expenditure relating to each individual property has to be considered in its own right, which can be very difficult if you're working on similar properties at the same time.

And just to make things even more complicated, sometimes businesses have to adjust the amount of VAT claimed in previous years. Under certain rules explained in this chapter, you may have to repay VAT you've already claimed, or if you may be entitled to claim ADDITIONAL VAT, because the situation changes or things didn't go to plan.

- Adjusting VAT claimed in previous years
- Clawback/payback or "change of use or intention
- Capital goods scheme

Adjusting VAT claimed in previous years

There are 2 procedures whereby you have to recalculate how much VAT you've claimed in previous years. They apply to all businesses, but for our purposes, we're really concerned about how they affect residential property developers.

They are known as the change of use or intention, known as the "clawback/payback" rules and the "capital goods scheme"; different procedures where you have to recalculate how much VAT you can claim on expenditure. This sometimes means that you have to repay some VAT tax to HMRC, or you may be able to claim more additional VAT in the following years, in some cases up to 10 years later.

The rules are complicated and may not affect your business, but it's important that you know that the rules exist even if you don't understand the rules in detail. I've explained the main principles below.

In both cases, the rules apply if you "change the use of goods or services" that you've bought. What does this mean?

In VAT terms, "change of use" normally means that you change the use from taxable to exempt supplies or vice versa. It sounds very technical, so we'll think about a real life situation about a property developer who has built a new house.

Rule 1: "Change of use" or "clawback/payback"

Scenario 1: The freehold sale of a new house by the developer is zero-rate if the conditions explained in Chapter 18 and VAT Notice 708, section 4, are met. Because the sale is "taxable at the zero-rate", the developer can claim the VAT on related costs.

Scenario 2: Short term residential lets, e.g. 6 month leases, are VAT exempt. Rent charged by our developer - see case study (see pages 73-76) is exempt, so the developer can't normally claim VAT on related costs.

Under the "clawback/payback" rules, the developer has to adjust VAT incurred on any costs within the previous 6 years if his plans change and he doesn't use the properties as originally anticipated.

Scenario 1 The developer can't sell the house so rents it out on short term lets. The income is exempt, instead of being zero-rated. This means that the developer has to repay some or all of the VAT originally claimed to HMRC. So in our case study our developer will have to repay some of the £9,750 VAT to represent the exempt rental income, although in practice the amount will probably be quite small.

Scenario 2 In the case study, our developer receives an offer to buy one of the flats before it's rented. The sale qualifies for the zero-rate so he can claim VAT that was previously unclaimed "exempt input tax". Going back to our case study, this means that he can claim the £5,600 VAT paid on the conversion.

The most common situation is that at Scenario 1, where house-builders can't sell new houses and have to rent them out before selling. In that case, house-builders will have to repay some of the VAT on costs, but in practice this is often a small amount.

Because of the volatility of the housing market, the clawback/payback provisions are probably more important for residential property developers than other business sectors. See Chapter 20 where I've discussed the special problems faced by house-builders.

Further information about the scheme is in HMRC VAT Notice 706: Partial exemption, section 13 http://tinyurl.com/nhv3rpo. Section 13.8 explains how the adjustments should be calculated.

Rule 2: Capital Goods Scheme ("CGS")

The CGS applies to VAT on property construction, purchases, leases and certain property costs such as extensions and renovations that cost £250,000 or more for use in a business up to 10 years AFTER the work has been carried out or the property acquired. It also applies to certain other "capital" goods, such as computer hardware, planes and boats.

Under the CGS, the business owner has to adjust VAT claims for up to 10 years after the property has been acquired or the work carried out. In practice, the CGS doesn't often apply to dwellings or other residential properties, because the construction and sale of new properties is zero-rated and reduced rated for conversion services. However the CGS could apply if, for example, there was a particularly expensive renovation or extension costing £250,000.

However to show how it works in practice, it's easiest to look at a commercial property. Let's assume that a property developer built an office block for £800,000 plus VAT £160,000.

- The developer let the property as an exempt supply for 2 years. This means that he couldn't claim any VAT on any of the construction costs because the property was generating exempt rental income.

- In year 3, the developer decided to "opt to tax" the property which means future rental income is liable to VAT at 20%. A new lease for a further 10 years is signed by the tenant. Because the developer has "opted to tax" the property, under the CGS rules, the developer can claim some of the VAT paid on the construction because the sale is taxable.

- The CGS applies over a 10 year period, so the developer can claim some of the VAT on the construction costs. Depending on the exact circumstances, the developer will be able to claim 80% of the VAT from HMRC at 10% each year; i.e. the proportion of the VAT on costs relating to the taxable rental income in years 3 - 10. This means that the developer can claim £16,000 from HMRC each year; a total of £132,000.

The CGS can be very difficult to manage, particularly if you're a commercial property owner with a lot of different properties. Thankfully it doesn't often affect residential property, but it's important to know about these things just in case.

Detailed guidance on the CGS is in VAT Notice 706/2: Capital Goods Scheme
http://tinyurl.com/pr5d3sy.

Chapter 19: Checklist

- As well as the normal partial exemption rules, businesses may have to recalculate how much VAT they can claim if things don't go to plan or developments in the future.
- The "change of intention" or "clawback/payback" provisions require businesses to adjust how much VAT they've claimed in the previous 6 years if they end up using a property for different purposes; especially letting new homes before selling them. This is the procedure most likely to affect residential property developers.
- Under the "capital goods scheme", businesses have to adjust how much VAT they can claim on costs during the 10 year period AFTER the initial construction/purchase/conversion.

Chapter 20

House-builders, converters and claiming VAT

One of the most commonly asked questions about claiming VAT by house-builders and convertors is the following:

We've claimed VAT on expenditure because we planned to sell our newly constructed/converted houses, but have had to let the properties first because we can't find buyers.

Do we have to pay the VAT back to HMRC?

Answer: probably yes, some of it, under "payback" rule which is explained in Chapter 19.

But working out how much can be quite complicated. And although this is one of the most commonly asked questions, **this is one of the most complex areas of VAT for house-builders and converters and probably the least understood by the business owners or their accountants**.

This is because the developers have to calculate the VAT under the "payback/clawback" rules explained in Chapter 19, under the procedures explained in VAT Notice 706, section 13.8 http://tinyurl.com/nhv3rpo.

In this chapter, I'll discuss the main issues for house-builders or developers who convert commercial property to dwellings in a bit more detail.

- HMRC's advice for house-builders: VAT Information Sheet 07/08
- VAT on costs and following basic principles
- VAT in the real world...

HMRC advice for house-builders and converters

HMRC are aware of the specific problems for house-builders caused by fluctuating housing market, particularly when things don't go to plan and when the construction/conversion work is carried out over a number of years. VAT Information Sheet 07/08: http://tinyurl.com/8jtu9sa was issued in 2008 to help house builders who receive exempt rental income before selling their properties to deal with partial exemption. I understand that this Information Sheet is still valid at the time of writing this book.

The Information Sheet explains that such businesses can use a "simple check for de minimis" for dealing with partial exemption in the first year in which they let the properties.

However this is a long and detailed Information Sheet, not easy to follow even for those of us with decades of VAT experience. But the principles may apply to you, depending on the circumstances.

In my experience, the most practical way of dealing with this situation is follow the basic principles set out in Notice 706, section 13.8 http://tinyurl.com/nhv3rpoto; based around the normal partial exemption method based on income. If you're in any doubt, or you would prefer to use a different method, you can write to HMRC with your proposals for a "special method" and ask them to confirm if they agree.

VAT on costs and following basic principles

There's no easy way to avoid dealing with these issues. But the best approach with most VAT issues is to keep things as simple as possible, whether you're dealing with the normal partial exemption procedures or calculating a clawback/payback adjustment. Most of this is by following basic principles, which I've summarized below.

- Keep your records up to date and allocate costs to specific properties as far as possible.
- If you're a developer, then you can try to keep things as simple as possible by working with the contractors to manage the VAT side of things.
- Remember that you can only claim VAT that has been correctly charged so it's important that you don't pay more than you should.
- Help your contractors correctly identify work that is eligible for the reduced rate or the zero-rate. Sometimes contractors overcharge VAT because of the risk that they will under charge VAT. This is understandable, because they have to pay VAT at the correct rate to HMRC whether or not they've charged the correct amount to their customers.
- As the customer in these situations, you can help by identifying the work which you believe should be charged at the reduced rate and including the information in the contract, so that the contractor. You can also help your contractor to minimize VAT by apportioning non-specific expenditure between standard rated, reduced rated and zero-rated work.
- Make sure that your contracts contain an agreed procedure for dealing with disputes about VAT liability of construction work; e.g. sharing the cost of asking for a ruling from HMRC or obtaining an opinion from an independent accountant or VAT consultant.
- Remember the basic partial exemption principle: that costs should be directly attributed to either taxable or exempt supplies. When we're dealing with property, this means

identifying which costs relate to which property so that the VAT recovery can be easily identified according to whether the property generates taxable income (i.e. zero-rated sale or holiday lets) or exempt income; i.e. short term residential lets.

VAT in the real world.....

As a VAT consultant, I understand the difficulties for developers, contractors and their accountants. The rules are complicated and we often spend a lot of time trawling through rules and regulations, writing long and detailed letters to asking HMRC to confirm if they agree with our proposed methods to calculate how much VAT you can claim from HMRC.

And even if you do your best to get it right, there's always the risk that HMRC will review your VAT records and may disagree with your application of the partial exemption rules or other issues. It's not just that you may have to pay an unexpected VAT bill, it's the sheer amount of time and hassle that you can spend dealing with complex VAT calculations.

VAT is particularly difficult for property developers because the business of property development doesn't fit easily into the VAT rules. Income and expenditure can be spread over a number of years and the value of rent or sales often doesn't represent how the goods and services are "used". Also, the standard partial exemption method is often distortive because the value of rent or sales doesn't represent how the goods and services are "used".

This is why property developers often opt to use special methods to calculate how much VAT they can claim because the standard partial exemption method doesn't allow for sufficiently accurate calculations for their business.

If you're a developer, you may need to apply for HMRC's permission to use a "special" partial exemption method that provides some flexibility for changing business circumstances, for example because the property market changes. But either way, you need to be a bit of a wizard to balance keeping things as simple as possible on the one hand, while ensuring you're claiming as much VAT as possible to keep your costs down.

In some cases it may be possible to ensure that you can claim VAT on property costs by setting up a separate leasing company for properties and selling any new/newly converted zero-rated to the leasing company. I'd strongly recommend that you take advice about these situations to ensure that things are done correctly. You also need to be certain that you're not doing anything that could be affected by any of the VAT anti-avoidance rules that can apply to transactions between associated businesses, particularly in respect of property and construction.

It would be good to finish on a positive note, but quite simply it's a difficult subject. The only silver lining in all of this is that you're in exactly the same boat as other property developers.

Chapter 20: Checklist

- The clawback/payback provisions explained in Chapter 19 can apply to house-builders or developers who claim VAT because they intend to sell new or newly converted dwellings.
- They must repay some or all of the VAT to HMRC if they let the property on an exempt lease before selling.
- If the developer intended to let the dwelling exempt from VAT and didn't claim any VAT on costs, but sells the freehold as a zero-rated sale before leasing, then the developer can claim some or all of the VAT from HMRC.
- The amount of VAT to be repaid or claimed calculated using the clawback/payback provisions explained in Chapter 19.
- The calculations can be complicated so it's a good idea to keeping things as simple as possible by following practical steps to avoid complex partial exemption calculations.

Chapter 21

Frequently asked questions and some answers!

Introduction to the FAQs:

- Why doesn't HMRC just write a list of everything that's zero-rated or reduced rated and everything that VAT registered contractors can claim?

- Why you need to get it right.

Section 1: Goods: building materials and installation

- Vanity units
- Electric gates and doors
- Integrated units
- Landscaping, plants, trees etc

Section 2: Services and other issues

- Detached garages
- Hiring equipment
- Scaffolding
- Plant and machinery
- Delivery

About this chapter and introduction to the FAQs

However much information is in this book or HMRC's guidance, chances are you'll have questions that aren't answered.

So in this chapter, I've discussed the most frequently asked questions about VAT for property developers and contractors to help point you in the right direction on a wide range of issues. Unfortunately, the answers aren't simply "yes" or "no" because the answer in each case depends on a number of factors unique to that subject. For example the factors about the VAT liability of vanity units supplied and installed by contractors are quite different to whether or not you can claim VAT on landscaping. Also, there are different issues to consider according to whether we're looking at new construction or conversions and renovations.

VAT registered property developers and VAT on expenditure

VAT registered property developers can normally ONLY claim VAT on goods and services used to make taxable supplies of residential property; including:

- zero-rated sales of new residential properties;
- zero-rated sales of non-residential conversions;
- zero-rated sales of substantially reconstructed listed buildings; and
- standard rated holiday lets.

References to claiming VAT in this chapter (21) are made on the assumption that the goods and services have been wholly used for the construction, conversion or reconstruction of such properties and that the properties have been sold as zero-rated supplies so that any VAT on expenditure is directly attributable to zero-rated sales. See Chapters 8 and 9 which deal with the VAT liability of income from properties.

But whether we're talking about vanity units or hiring scaffolding, there are 2 main factors:

- how much VAT you have to pay on the cost; and
- whether you can claim the VAT on your VAT return.

For each question, I've explained the main issues and also given my opinion of the correct liability of the construction work and whether you can claim the VAT for either new construction and conversions - see the "VAT Implications" summary at the end of each section. However please understand that every situation is unique and the VAT implications in your case may be different, even if the circumstances seem to be very similar.

- In each case, I've explained <u>when contractors should charge VAT on the supply and installation of the goods or materials</u> concerned, according to whether the goods/materials qualify as "building materials".
- You'll pay 20% VAT on any goods bought from a supplier who doesn't install the goods.
- Remember that developers can't claim VAT on goods unless those goods are "building materials", even if the sale of the new or newly converted property will be zero-rated.
- The "VAT claim" summary confirms whether the VAT on the goods and/or services can be claimed as input tax on VAT returns.
- Finally, even if your specific issue isn't covered in this chapter, I'd suggest that you read the chapter anyway because it should help you to work out the VAT treatment in your own situation.

<u>N.B.</u> I'm sure that some of you will have different interpretations of the rules; or you may even have received a completely different ruling from HMRC. I'm always interested to hear of any alternative rulings or opinions on these issues so please let me know if you have any such information.

Section 1: Goods: Building Materials

Remember: if you buy goods direct - as opposed to paying a contractor to supply AND install the goods - then you have to pay 20% VAT. You can only claim this VAT if the goods are building materials.

However, as explained in Chapters 11 -12, *your contractor can charge the zero-rate or reduced rate for "building materials" that are supplied and installed by the contractor in the course of new construction and qualifying conversions and renovations*. Building materials include everything from basic stuff like bricks and mortar to fitted kitchen furniture, as explained in Chapter 15.

However it's not always easy to work out whether certain goods are regarded as "building materials", simply because there are so many different types of expenditure. And there is still a lot of confusion about certain common types of expenditure, including vanity units, electric gates and plants and trees, all of which I've discussed in this chapter.

Also, sometimes the VAT liability of the goods is different to the service element, or labour of installing the goods.

Here's a good example: suppose your contractor is installing an electric oven. The oven itself doesn't qualify as "building materials" so the contractor has to charge VAT on his charge for the oven.

However, if the contractor installs the oven in the course of constructing a new dwelling, the labour element (or services) for fitting the oven will be zero-rated, as long as the zero-rated/reduced rated supplies are identified separately on his invoice.

So where do you start? First, you need to establish whether the goods are "building materials" as discussed in Chapter 15.

Here are the main criteria:

- The articles are incorporated into the buildings (or its site)
- the articles are "ordinarily" incorporated by builders into that type of building

- other than kitchen furniture, the articles are not finished or prefabricated furniture, or materials for the construction of fitted furniture
- with certain exceptions, the articles are not gas or electrical appliances
- the articles are not carpets or carpeting material

See Chapter 15 and VAT Notice 708, paragraph 13 http://tinyurl.com/n6gttof.

The goods must meet ALL of the criteria to qualify as "building materials".

You might think that HMRC's list is based around the difference between "basic" goods and more "luxury" items, but in fact the rules are set out in the legislation. HMRC has to administer the rules and has little lee-way when it comes to interpretation. However a lot of the issues, e.g. the meaning of "vanity unit" and VAT on landscaping a new home, have been considered by the VAT/Tax Tribunal so we can find some very helpful guidance from the court decisions.

1.1   Vanity units

One of the most common queries is about "vanity units" and whether they fall within the category of "furniture". If they are furniture, then they aren't "building materials".

So what exactly is a "vanity unit"?

HMRC's guidance in Notice 708, paragraph 13.5.2(b) http://tinyurl.com/n6gttof explains that building materials includes the following:

"items that provide storage capacity as an incidental result of their primary function, such as shelves formed as a result of constructing simple box work over pipes, and basin supports which contain a simple cupboard beneath, ..."

In other words, a cupboard with shelves under a sink or surrounding a pedastal or pipework.This It also includes deeper units incorporating a wash hand basin installed in bathrooms, cloakrooms and bedrooms, as long as *the only cupboard space is directly beneath the basin itself.* For the purposes of this book, I'll refer to this as a "basic vanity unit".

However, building materials DO NOT include "elaborate vanity units", which include those where the basic unit is part of a larger unit, for example, where additional units are constructed either side of the basin, as well as wall units with bathroom cabinets.

I've set out the VAT implications for both "basic vanity units" and "elaborate vanity units" below.

VAT implications for basic vanity unit

What rate of VAT should the contractor charge?

- New construction: the supply of the goods would be zero-rated and the services qualify for zero-rating as part of new construction.
- Qualifying conversions and renovations: reduced rate for both goods and services.

Can VAT registered developers claim VAT?

- New construction: VAT registered developers cannot claim any VAT charged in new construction, because the contractor should zero-rate their supply and installation.
- VAT registered developers can claim VAT on both goods and services in conversions charged at the reduced rate.

VAT implications for "elaborate vanity unit"

What rate of VAT should the contractor charge?

- New construction: the supply of the goods would be standard rated, but the labour/services will qualify for zero-rating as part of new construction.
- Qualifying conversions and renovations: both the goods/materials and services are liable to the standard rate; i.e. 20%.

Can VAT registered developers claim VAT?

- New construction: VAT registered developers cannot claim any VAT charged for materials/goods in new construction because the goods are not "building materials". The services of installation should be zero-rated.
- Sales of non-residential conversions: VAT registered developers cannot claim VAT on the materials/goods in conversions because they are not "building materials", but can normally claim VAT charged at 20% on the services of installing the elaborate vanity unit.

1.2 Electrically operated garage doors, gates and electrical components.

Another common area of confusion is that of electrically operated garage doors and gates.

VAT Notice 708, paragraph 13.6 explains that certain types of electronic items aren't regarded as "building materials" because they aren't "ordinarily installed" in dwellings. These include:

"electrical components for garage doors and gates (including remote controls)"

In practice, I take this to mean that <u>manual</u> gates and garage doors are normally regarded as "building materials". However if you subsequently add electronic components to make the gates or the doors electronically operated, then the components aren't regarded as "building materials". I also understand that HMRC does not regard electrically powered gates or garage doors as "building materials", although this is not covered in Notice 708.

The VAT implications set out below refer to both electrically powered gates and garage doors supplied during the course of construction, renovations and conversions, as well as electrical components added to garage doors and gates during renovations and conversions.

<u>VAT implications for electrically powered gates and garage doors and electronic components added to manual gates or doors</u>

What rate of VAT should the contractor charge?

- New construction: the goods would be standard rated but the labour would qualify for zero-rating as part of new construction.
- Qualifying conversions and renovations: standard rate for both goods and services.

Can VAT registered developers claim VAT ?

- New construction: VAT registered developers cannot claim for goods in new construction because the goods aren't building materials. Any services should qualify for zero-rated as part of the new construction.
- Sales of non-residential conversions: VAT registered developers can't claim VAT on the materials/goods in conversions because they are not "building materials", but can normally claim VAT charged at 20% on the services of installing the elaborate vanity unit.

1.3   Integrated appliances

There are so many different types of appliances nowadays that it would be impossible for HMRC to provide a definitive list of whether such items are "building materials.

In the case of integrated appliances, there are 2 main criteria to consider:

- Is the item "incorporated" into the building; and
- is it one of the "gas or electrical appliances" that are defined as "building materials?

Let's consider two different appliances: a boiler and an oven. Assume that both are built-in to the property, wired-in and (in the case of the boiler) plumbed in. The oven is not attached to any other type of heating module or boiler.

One of the criteria to be "building materials" is that integrated electronic or gas items are only included if they are "*designed by the manufacturer to heat space or water (this includes cookers which are designed to have a dual purpose to heat the room or the building's water)*" VAT Notice 708, paragraph 13.6 http://tinyurl.com/n6gttof.

However in Notice 708, paragraph 13.9, HMRC also says:
Please note that cookers cannot be considered to be 'space heaters' just because they incidentally radiate heat while operating. To be classified as 'designed to heat space or water, they must be fitted to a heating module or boiler. http://tinyurl.com/n6gttof

So where does this leave our boiler and cooker?

Boiler

The boiler is clearly designed to heat water so qualifies as a "building material".

Cooker

Although the cooker is wired-in, it isn't linked to any heating module or boiler. It doesn't qualify as a water heater or space heater, even though the heat from the oven causes the kitchen to heat up while in use.

VAT implications for the boiler

What rate of VAT should the contractor charge?

- New construction: The supply and installation of the boiler would qualify for zero-rating as part of new construction.
- Qualifying conversions and renovations : the supply and installation of the boiler would qualify for the reduced rate.

Can VAT registered developers claim VAT?

- New construction: VAT registered developers selling new construction. The supply and installation services in the course of construction of a new dwelling should qualify for zero-rating as part of new construction so the developer can't claim any VAT charged.
- Sales of non-residential conversions: VAT registered developers selling non-residential conversion can claim VAT charged at 5% on both the boiler and any charge for installation in conversions.

VAT implications for the cooker

What rate of VAT should the contractor charge?

- New construction The supply of the cooker would be standard rated but the labour may qualify for zero-rating if the cooker is supplied and installed in the course of the new construction.
- Qualifying conversions and renovations: both the cooker and the installation charge would be standard rated.

Can VAT registered developers claim VAT?

- New construction: VAT registered developers cannot claim VAT on the purchase of the cooker because it is not "building materials". The contractor should not charge VAT on its installation.
- Sales of non-residential conversions: VAT registered developers can't claim VAT on the materials/goods in conversions because they are not "building materials", but can normally claim VAT charged at 20% on the services of installation.

1.4   Landscaping, trees, plants etc

Another subject that causes a lot of confusion is whether trees, plants, soil, turf and other goods used in landscaping are "building materials". The rules for new construction are different to those for conversions and renovations.

New construction

Under the rules, the zero-rate or DIY claim can only apply to the extent that the services and goods used in the course of those services that are "closely connected" to the construction of the building itself. HMRC accept that some landscaping is "closely connected" to the new construction, which means that certain garden materials and plants qualify as "building materials".

This normally means that the contractor can only zero-rate part of the cost of the supply and installation of the goods and VAT registered developers can't claim VAT on all of the goods. As with any other "mixed" supply, if the contractor doesn't identify goods and services that are zero-rated, then the whole of the supply is liable to the standard rate and DIY claimants will not be able to claim any of the VAT.

However, in addition to the usual factors, there's also an additional rule that relates specifically to trees, plants and shrubs detailed on landscaping schemes as explained below.

Guidance in VAT Notice 708: http://tinyurl.com/n6gttof

Paragraph 13.8.2 confirms that building materials includes the following:

"turf, topsoil, grass seed, plants and trees (but please note that trees, shrubs and plants are only 'building materials in particular circumstances - see para 3.3.4)"

Paragraph 3.3.4 says:

Please note that the planting of shrubs, trees and flowers would not normally be seen as being 'closely connected...' ***except to the extent that it is detailed on a landscaping scheme approved by a planning authority under the terms of a planning consent condition.*** *This does not include the replacement of trees and shrubs that die, or become damaged or diseased.*

In other words:

- the planting of topsoil, turf and plants "closely connected" to the dwelling is zero-rated and the goods concerned are "building materials";

- any work done outside the "closely connected" areas is standard rated and the goods are not "building materials";

- in either situation, the planting of trees, plants and shrubs is only regarded as "closely connected" if ***is detailed on a landscaping scheme approved by a planning authority under the terms of a planning consent condition.***

Example

Here's an example of a typical scenario and how I think the rules apply in practical terms.

In practice, there are 2 steps: first you have to identify whether the work is "closely connected" to the construction of the new property; second remember that planting trees, shrubs and plants ONLY falls within the remit of "closely connected if *is detailed on a landscaping scheme approved by a planning authority under the terms of a planning consent condition.*

Suppose there is a new house under construction with a 50 foot garden, much of which includes lawn, trees and various plants. In this case, the trees, plants and shrubs are detailed on the landscaping scheme that has been approved by the local planning authority under the terms of a planning consent condition.

HMRC would normally agree that a proportion of the services of creating the garden and the goods are "closely connected" where the garden immediately surrounds the house. But what proportion?

In this case, there's a footpath situated about 6 feet around the outside of the house which enables people to access the property. Between the footpath and the house, there is a strip of grass and some flower beds.

The supply and installation of the topsoil, grass, plants and trees would be as follows:

- new construction: the installation of topsoil, planting grass seed or turf between the path and the house would probably be regarded as "building materials" and therefore zero-rated:

- anything outside that area is not "building materials", so the goods and the services are both standard rated.

This is a messy subject and also a bit subjective - your interpretation of "closely connected" may be different to HMRC's interpretation. To avoid hassle and also to keep your VAT costs down, I'd suggest that you need to agree in advance with the contractor/landscaper about the proportion of the goods/plants etc that are liable to VAT and what proportion of the services are liable to VAT. Ensure that the zero-rated goods and services are separately identified on the invoices. If you're still in doubt, your contractor can ask HMRC for a ruling on the issue.

Renovations and conversions

Unfortunately, the reduced rate for work done on gardens in the course of renovations or conversions are less generous than the reliefs for new homes. For example, the reduced rate doesn't extend to any landscaping services. This means that the reduced rate does not apply to any of the goods involved; plants, seeds, topsoil etc.

<u>VAT implications</u>

What rate of VAT should the contractor charge?

- New construction : the supply and installation of turf, topsoil, grass seed, plants and trees can normally be zero-rated if "closely connected" to the construction of the property. However the supply and installation of the planting of trees, shrubs and flowers are only zero-rated if detailed on a landscaping scheme approved a planning authority under the terms of a planning consent condition.
- Qualifying conversions and renovations: Standard rate for both goods and services.

Can VAT registered developers claim VAT ?

- New construction: VAT registered developers can only claim VAT on plants and trees in new construction if they qualify as "building materials" as explained above. VAT cannot be claimed on any gardening/landscaping services that qualify for the zero-rate.
- Sales of non-residential conversions: VAT registered developers can't claim VAT on the cost of any goods: plants, turf, soil etc; or services.

Section 2: Services and other issues

I've discussed below some other common problem areas not related to building materials, including how the rules apply to detached garages, as well as scaffolding and plant hire.

2.1   Detached garages.

There is a lot of confusion about the treatment of detached buildings within the grounds of dwellings. Usually, construction of separate buildings that don't form part of the dwelling is standard rated, for example HMRC specifically say that a swimming pool that is in a separate building doesn't count as the construction of a new dwelling.   VAT Notice 708, paragraph 3.2.2 http://tinyurl.com/mdc8465 says:

"*This is because the building being constructed is not 'a building designed as a dwelling' ...*"

The same principles would also apply to other outbuildings such as barns or stables because those buildings aren't "designed as a dwelling".

However the rules about detached garages are different.

The normal rules are that *garages, whether detached or physically linked, are treated as part of the dwelling as long as the garage is intended to be used with the dwelling and any work on the garage is carried out at the same time as the main construction, conversion or renovation.*

This means that the construction of a garage, whether detached or physically linked, in the course of the construction of a dwelling is zero-rated, along with the building materials used in its construction.

The reduced rate also applies to work carried out on garages in the course of qualifying conversions and renovations as explained in Chapters 12 and 13.

What rate of VAT should the contractor charge?

* New construction: construction of a new garage in the course of the construction of a new dwelling is zero-rated.

- Qualifying conversions and renovations: construction of a new garage, conversion of a building into a garage and renovation of a garage, in the course of a qualifying conversion or renovation is reduced rated - see VAT Notice 708, paragraphs 7.6.1 and 8.4.1.

Can VAT registered developers claim VAT?

- New construction: VAT registered developers can't claim VAT on goods or services because their supply by contractors should be zero-rated.
- Sales of non-residential conversions: VAT registered developers can claim VAT charged at the reduced rate on the services and materials used to construct or carry out work on a garage in the course of a qualifying conversion.

2.2   Plant and machinery

The hire of plant and machinery without an operator is standard-rated.

However, if you hire plant and machinery with an operator, then the nature of the service changes. It's no longer regarded as the hire of goods, but how the operator uses the plant/machinery; for example demolition, site clearance etc. Therefore, in certain circumstances, the supply of plant/machinery with an operator in the course of the construction of a dwelling can be zero-rated. See VAT Notice 708, paragraphs 3.1.2 and 3.4.2 http://tinyurl.com/mdc8465.

The reduced rate can also apply to the hire of plant and machinery with an operator if and only to the extent that it relates to qualifying services in the course of a qualifying conversion or renovation, as explained in Chapter 12 and VAT Notice 708, paragraphs 7 and 8. However the reduced rate is limited to qualifying services; i.e. work done to the fabric of the property and certain services within the immediate site (in connection with the provision of water, power, security, etc).

What rate of VAT should the contractor charge?

- New construction: the supply of the plant or machinery with an operator can be zero-rated when the services are provided in the course of the construction of a zero rated building.
- Qualifying conversions and renovations: the supply of the plant or machinery with an operator can be reduced rated if supplied in the course of reduced rated conversions and renovations.

Can VAT registered developers claim VAT?

- New construction: VAT registered developers can claim VAT on the hire of plant/machinery without an operator in new construction. If supplied with an operator, VAT should not be charged as the service forms part of the zero-rated new construction.
- Sales of non-residential conversions: VAT registered developers can claim VAT on the hire of plant/machinery without an operator in conversions. If supplied with an operator, VAT at the reduced rate should be charged as the service forms part of the reduced rated "qualifying services" heading.

2.3   Scaffolding

The hire of any equipment on its own is always liable to VAT at the standard rate, including scaffolding, formwork and falsework, and machinery.

However if the scaffolding or machinery is supplied with labour in the course of new construction, then the provision of the labour element for the erection and dismantling of scaffolding in the course of new construction can be zero-rated; see VAT Notice 708, paragraphs 3.1.2 and 3.4.2 http://tinyurl.com/mdc8465.

If you hire scaffolding and the labour to erect and dismantle the scaffolding from the same supplier, then the supplier can apportion their charge and zero-rate the amount relating to the labour element. But if they charge a single amount then the entire charge is liable to VAT at the standard rate.

The service of erecting or dismantling scaffolding in the course of conversions and renovations is liable to the standard rate; see VAT Notice 708, paragraphs 7.6 and 8.6.

What rate of VAT should the contractor charge?

- New construction: hire of scaffolding on its own is standard rated. The supply of the labour to erect or dismantle scaffolding may qualify for zero-rating when provided in the course of the construction of a zero rated building: see VAT Notice 708, paragraphs 3.1.2 and 3.4.2 http://tinyurl.com/mdc8465.
- Qualifying conversions and renovations: both the hire of scaffolding and the supply of the labour to erect or dismantle scaffolding in the course of conversions and renovations are standard rated.

Can VAT registered developers claim VAT?

- New construction: VAT registered developers in new construction can claim VAT correctly charged on the hire of scaffolding in the course of new construction.
- Sales of non-residential conversions: VAT registered developers can claim VAT correctly charged on both the hire of scaffolding or the labour costs.

2.4   Delivery charges

Delivery charges for goods in the UK are normally liable to VAT at the standard rate - see VAT Notice 700, The VAT Guide, section 8.3 http://tinyurl.com/lvbpnsr

VAT on delivery charges can be claimed under the normal VAT rules.

What rate of VAT should the contractor charge?

- New construction: If the delivery of the goods is included in the cost of the supply and installation of building materials in the course of the construction of a new dwelling, then the whole cost is zero-rated. Otherwise delivery is standard rated.
- Qualifying conversions and renovations: If the delivery of the goods is included in the cost of the supply and installation of building materials in the course of a qualifying construction or renovation, then the whole cost is liable to the reduced rate. Otherwise delivery is standard rated.

Can VAT registered developers claim VAT?

- New construction: VAT registered developers: Yes if correctly charged.
- Sales of non-residential conversions: VAT registered developers: Yes if correctly charged.

Chapter 22: The 3 step process

If you're reading this page, chances are that you've skipped through a lot of the detailed information just to get a sense of the content of the book.

And that's absolutely fine - even as a VAT consultant, I'd find it a challenge to read a whole lot of detailed technical stuff. However much I try to make the subject practical and relevant, at the end of the day, it does come down to dealing with a lot of detailed VAT laws. It's easy to be overwhelmed with so much information, which is why it's important to keep focused on the big picture so you understand when and why the more detailed stuff applies.

Step 1: How will the finished property be used?
You need to know the type of property you're developing and what you plan to do with it so that you can work out the VAT liability of the sales or rental income - see Chapters 7 and 8 for information about this.

Step 2: What sort of property are you creating/converting?
If the end result of your construction or conversion is a dwelling or other "qualifying property", or you're renovating an empty dwelling, the contractors' services and related goods may qualify for either the zero-rate for new construction or the reduced rate for certain conversions and renovations. See Chapters 10 - 15 for information about saving VAT on costs.

Step 3: How much VAT can you claim from HMRC?
The final part of the process is how much VAT you can claim from HMRC, which depends on the VAT liability of the income from the sales and or leases of the new/converted property. It often means that developers have to deal with the difficult subject of partial exemption and re-calculating VAT claimed in previous years. See Chapters 18 - 20.

Once you get your head around the main principles, you'll find that you start to understand where the more detailed rules fit into the big picture and that you've a much better idea of how to work out the right VAT cost from the beginning. You'll be able to identify potential VAT savings for additional profit AND when you have to budget for additional VAT costs, so you can you plan properly, save time and reduce the hassle and stress of dealing with HMRC.

You don't need to be an expert all at once; just understand how the main issues fit together.

Appendix 1: HMRC Public Notices

VAT Notice 700: The VAT Guide http://tinyurl.com/9ykqw.

VAT Notice 700/1: Should I be registered for VAT?: http://tinyurl.com/396kxa.

VAT Notice 701/1: Charities: http://tinyurl.com/2tnfm3.

VAT Notice 708: Buildings and construction: http://tinyurl.com/ez77v.

VAT Notice 709/3: Hotels and holiday accommodation: http://tinyurl.com/k3pdedg.

VAT Notice 742a: Opting to tax land and buildings: http://tinyurl.com/3g32uz.

VAT Notice 742/3: Scottish land law terms: http://tinyurl.com/br4gq57

Appendix 2: Definitions

Dwellings

Definition 1: "Designed as a dwelling or number of dwellings"

This applies where a building contains a dwelling or more than one dwelling **and** each dwelling meets the following conditions:

- the dwelling consists of self-contained living accommodation;
- there is no provision for direct internal access from the dwelling to any other dwelling or part of a dwelling;
- the separate use of the dwelling is not prohibited by the terms of any covenant, statutory planning consent or similar provision;
- the separate disposal of the dwelling is not prohibited by the terms of any covenant, statutory planning consent or similar provision; and
- statutory planning consent has been granted in respect of that dwelling and its construction or conversion has been carried out in accordance with that consent.

When does this definition apply?

Chapter 7: zero-rated construction of new dwellings.

Chapter 20: zero-rated sales of, or long leases in, new dwellings and in, non-residential conversions.

Definition 2: "Designed to remain as or become a dwelling or number of dwellings"

This applies where a building contains a dwelling or more than one dwelling **and** each dwelling meets the following conditions:

- the dwelling consists of self-contained living accommodation;
- there is no provision for direct internal access from the dwelling to any other dwelling or part of a dwelling;
- the separate use of the dwelling is not prohibited by the terms of any covenant, statutory planning consent or similar provision; and
- the separate disposal of the dwelling is not prohibited by the terms of any covenant, statutory planning consent or similar provision.

When does this definition apply?

Chapter 20: zero-rated sale of substantially reconstructed listed buildings.

Definition 3: "Single household dwelling"

Any dwelling that meets the following conditions:

- is designed for occupation by a single household either as a result of having been originally constructed for that purpose (and has not been subsequently adapted for occupation of any other kind), or as a result of adaptation;
- consists of self-contained living accommodation;
- has no provision for direct internal access to any other dwelling or part of a dwelling;
- is not prohibited from separate use by the terms of any covenant, statutory planning consent or similar provision; and
- is not prohibited from separate disposal by the terms of any covenant, statutory planning consent or similar provision.

Definition 4: "Multi-occupancy dwelling"

This means any dwelling that meets the following conditions:

- is designed for occupation by persons not forming a single household either as a result of having been originally constructed for that purpose (and has not been subsequently adapted for occupation of any other kind), or as a result of adaptation;
- is not to any extent used for a relevant residential purpose;
- consists of self-contained living accommodation;
- has no provision for direct internal access from the dwelling to any other dwelling or part of a dwelling;
- is not prohibited from separate use by the terms of any covenant, statutory planning consent or similar provision; and
- is not prohibited from separate disposal by the terms of any covenant, statutory planning consent or similar provision.

When do these definitions apply?

Chapters 2 and 8:

- Reduced rated conversions of properties to different number of single household dwellings.
- Reduced rated renovations of existing dwellings which have been unoccupied for 2 years or longer.

Index

25838052R00114

Printed in Poland
by Amazon Fulfillment
Poland Sp. z o.o., Wrocław